Sod's Law
of the Sea

Sod's Law of the Sea

Bill Lucas
Andrew Spedding

STANFORD MARITIME

Stanford Maritime Limited
Member Company of the George Philip Group
59 Grosvenor St, London W1X 9DA

First published in Great Britain 1977
Reprinted 1977, 1978, 1979, 1980, 1982, 1983, 1984, 1987,
1988
Copyright © William Lucas and Andrew Spedding 1977
Drawings © Andrew Spedding 1977

Photoset in 10/11 English Times

Printed in Great Britain by
J W Arrowsmith Limited, Bristol.

ISBN 0 540 07175 7

Introduction

Sod's Law is a well known theorem which proclaims that a slice of bread buttered and jammed aspect UP, will, if dropped, land on the rug aspect DOWN.

At sea it also lands aspect DOWN, but also at sea an inverted bottom and legs indicate that the top end of that person is hanging down through the open floor cover over the engine trying to stop the shaft turning. A lurch from the boat divorces the slice of bread from the adhesive sticking it to the floor: the bread slides past the engineer. As it goes past his right ear he tries to grab it, misses, swears, and drops the spanner in the sump and swears harder.

The cussing from the engine alarms the cook out of the galley space; she steps on, and slides with, the remaining butter and jam. On deck the crew are handing the spinnaker which they hurl down the hatch on top of the jam, the engineer, the cook and the pot full of greasy stew she had been holding prior to the incident. A keen young foredeck hand rushes down to the saloon to get out a new headsail. As he clambers over the heap of red nylon he does not notice that it conceals two muttering fellow crew members, or for that matter the open engine cover. He falls and helps push the mess into the engine space where the exhaust pipe, still hot from a battery charge, burns a hole in the spinnaker. The coaming edge claims a slice of his shin. Someone on deck shouts 'Now the workers have got the kite off, how about some grub?'

It takes some time to sort out the shambles in the saloon, and in the process the bread that slid into the bilge is forgotten. Four hours later the new watch pump the bilge, and the offending slice is turned into bread paste and jams the outlet valve on the pump. The engine hatch is again lifted to attend to the pump when someone coming off watch carves himself a thick wad of bread, butters it, and spreads half a pot of strawberry jam over the top, then. . . .

This book has nothing whatsoever to do with this concept. You will see in the hereafter that my Uncle Adrian Spindrift-Smith's initials were memorable, but that he was not known by them. In a rather private war in the Adriatic he had over two years done his best to deny as many home comforts to the nearby German army as possible. Ten days before he left that theatre, bureaucracy caught up with him and he was listed as Senior Officer Dubrovnic. S.O.D. SMITH stuck. SOD'S LAW OF THE SEA it is.

Uncle Adrian's Instructions

There are many books on sailing instruction and the use of the sea. This does not purport to be one of them.

After a distinguished, if not notorious, career in and out of the Navy, and many years' hard offshore sailing, my illustrious Uncle Adrian poured himself out of a meeting of friends at a very senior Yacht Club. At the top of the landing his feet had a very nasty port and starboard collision with the steward's black Siamese cat. The resulting fall down the main staircase demolished the balustrade and smashed to pieces a large mahogany cabinet and the enclosed large model of a J Class yacht which had been a mid-30s plucky effort to wrestle the America's Cup from its home in New York.

What Uncle said was not recorded, except by the cat, which thereafter became neurotic and had to be put down. In spite of being anesthetized before the casualty, Uncle Adrian sustained serious injury which paralysed him from the waist downwards.

The oil company for whom he consulted were sympathetic in public and damned glad to be shot of him in private, and made him a monumental settlement. The combination of circumstances caused Uncle Adrian to flee as soon as he was allowed by the Matron of Osborne House to a climate of cheaper gin, warmer weather and cooler taxation. He decided to inflict himself on the island of Malta.

Although I had been weaned on the salty fare of Arthur Ransome, Slocum and Hornblower as well as others of a traditional British Seamanlike heritage, my designated role in life did not seem to present many opportunities to shine as a latter-day Hawkins. My commitment to a family insurance business in a cathedral town had constricted my sailing in both time and finance, and at the time of Adrian's Fall had involved only the fortnight at the sailing school in Scotland, when I had learned little on the two days in the fortnight it had not been blowing a full gale. I took a girlfriend for a trip on the Norfolk Broads and my experience aptly confirmed most of the predictions of Michael Green, but this had excited the interest and I had bought a little outboard cruiser which I was then keeping on the Kennet & Avon Canal; the longest voyage until then had been to Reading and back.

Most families have a real or imagined 'black sheep' and I suppose Uncle Adrian was ours. When my parents selected him as my Godfather he was still young enough in their opinion to reform, but as he had not done so they spent the next thirty years successfully keeping his benign influence out of my life. While I was never quite certain why he was regarded as such an ogre, gossip between Great Aunts had certainly impressed on my young mind that he was different. I can promise you that anyone who had pinched my Great Aunt Rebecca's bottom *was* different, and while this might once have pleased her, the fact that it had happened in the family pew in the Wesleyan Chapel made it a crime of unforgiveable proportions. She in turn was strong on Temperance, and both Adrian's mode of life and the fact that when her father had passed on she felt it proper to pour a cellar full of very good port and chateau wine down the scullery sink had created an irretrievable breach. Only Aunt Enid maintained secret contact with the nephew she had secretly adored all her life. As far as I know I had not seen or been seen by Uncle Adrian since the time he had slipped into a pew rather late in the Christening service and undertaken to see to my religious education.

It therefore came as a profound shock to receive the following letter from him in February 1971.

St Paul's Bay, Malta

Dear David,

I am your godfather, and your mother's cousin. Disregard everything the family have to say about me.

Your Aunt Enid tells me that you are keen on sailing, but are held on a leash by the family necessity to insure the good burghers of Cirencester. Sailing will do you more good than insurance, and in any case if you want to do any real insurance you will find the best place to find the Committee of Lloyds is on the Solent and not off Gracechurch Street.

You may have heard that I fell over and wrecked my legs and am told that I will be stuck in this damned chair until I drink myself stupid. I have never known a quack to be right yet, and until I make up my mind if they could be right I would be grateful if you would sail *Lassitude* for me. She is a 54 ft ketch and is now wintering in St Malo. Keep her going and do a bit of racing. A chap called Nigel on 629-0076 can usually drum up a bit of a crew. The effort is not within your pocket, but Gordon at the Haymarket branch of Coutts has been instructed to put you in funds for petty cash and to meet the yard bills.

Don't dream of not accepting, have a good time, and let me know how you get on.

ADRIAN SPINDRIFT-SMITH

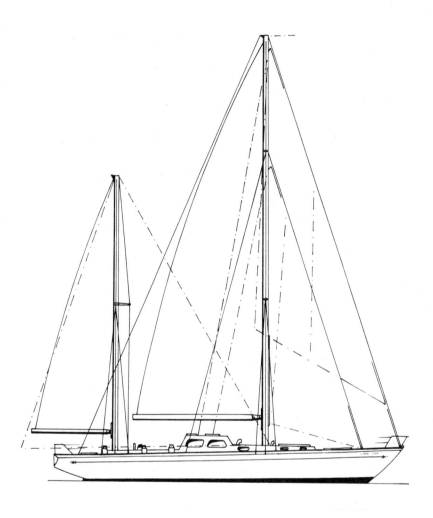

Lassitude *54' L.O.A. ketch. Xanthoxylum planking on gaboon frames. Designer Hamish Buttercup of Gribble, Giles & Borer in 1960(?) Expensively (and often unintentionally) modified by her crew. Rerigged: often. Sails: Ripstop & Luffem. Spars: Sheer & Derrick. Builders: Chipping Sodbury Boat Construction Co.*

At the age of thirty most people know their limitations, and I knew mine to be bound by the horizons of the family business in a large market town. The appeal was irresistible.

In the years since that letter I have sailed *Lassitude* about 15,000 miles and learned to sail a bit. Very sadly, Uncle Adrian proved the exception to his rule about doctors and stayed in his wheelchair. As he said, he had more income than he could drink, and I think those years have been enlivened for him by regular letters about his boat and those who sailed in her. In return he wrote many, many letters of encouragement, discipline, query and instruction.

These letters form the basis of this book, and are not quite the sort of instruction you can get from a seamanship manual of a more conventional style. As the letters were not written for publication, and Adrian's prose stayed free, the laws of libel and standards of publishing taste have required some drastic editing, and some gems of information are collected in rough order. Deference to his surviving wives or any children he would speak of have required some changed names, his included, but if you know the man behind the ruse, or think that you are one of the characters, please realize that the overall message is that Sailing Is Fun before you instruct your solicitor.

David Creeper
Cowes 1977

The substance of these letters will of course reveal something of the Character of Adrian Spindrift-Smith. In spite of very generous offers from the family a short biography may help to set the scene.

A. Spindrift-Smith, born Southsea 1906, the third son of Amelia S.S. and Cdr. S.S., R.N. Gossips of the Naval society into which he was born noted that he had gestated rather longer than usual, his father having left Southsea for service on the West Indies Station eleven months before his arrival. The given name by his mother which resulted in a mnemonic of his initials being easily remembered may have reflected this unjust persecution.

In 1919 he followed form by entering R.N. College Dartmouth to begin the Naval programme of (a) developing his Individual Initiative and Character and (b) achieving (a) within the limitations of a disciplined Service. It is fair to say that they succeeded well at (a) and failed dismally at (b).

As a young Sub in 1923 S.S. first got his name noted by the Board of Admiralty by having attempted to wave to a girlfriend on the deck of the outward-bound *Empress of Canada*. The low pass he made over the funnel proved disastrous, however, and the downdraft in its shadow caused him to crash-land on No. 4 deck tennis court. The biplane had a range of 120 miles and the Admiralty had to pay for it and its driver to be shipped back from New York.

By 1926 he had succeeded in a competitive Service of being very well known indeed when, in addition to his normal indiscretions of an odd grounding, a close miss at the target plane instead of the towed target, and other sins a developing Service know how to forgive, he committed an unforgiveable one with the wife of a well connected flag captain, and had the added misfortune to do so in a hired Dhiso which was passed at high speed and close quarters by a destroyer taking the C-in-C for a swimming party off Sicily. By what is now known as a unilateral decision the Navy List and S.S. parted company.

The years up to the war are confusing but were mostly spent in the Far East. He became a partner in an interesting company which traded as the Hong Kong & Wusan Steamship Company, married twice and became an Extra Master Mariner, surveyed a chunk of the South China Sea, laid some telegraph cable, and did a couple of salvage jobs. His name still commands respect in the Peninsular Hotel, and one way or another he seems to have made a modest fortune.

The war caught him unwisely taking a third honeymoon in Austria, and he had to walk a good part of the way home. He found the Admiralty in a reasonably forgiving mood, and war is such that it provided scope for his talents to an extent that in six years he was rewarded with one Court Martial, two Courts of Inquiry, a D.S.O. and Bar.

After a year in post-war England Uncle somehow managed to obtain a job with the Colonial Office as an Assistant Resident attached to the ruler of Lesser Arabia, Sheikh Mohamed Arwal. He advised the ruler on Foreign Affairs relating to his very large chunk of sand, 10,000 population and village capital, and at the same time ran by far the fastest sailing dhow in the Persian Gulf and taught the ruler the rudiments of backgammon, liar dice and mahjong.

Discovery of heavy oil reserves in the State of Lesser Arabia caused the Foreign Office to feel that a divorce of Adrian and his backgammon partner was desirable. The Sheikh, however, did not agree having almost got used to Adrian. It took a massive bribe in the form of a consultancy agreement from the interested oil company to winkle Adrian out, and the terms suited both of them. Under no circumstances was Adrian to consult about anything. He went sailing instead.

The letters make more sense when some of the incidents which caused them or were caused by them are also related. In the event most of the crew I inherited stayed with the act. As what they had to say about some of A.S.S.'s exploits is relevant to what he subsequently wrote, I think it wise to first mention some of the principal characters on *Lassitude*.

Brigadier Erstwhile-Paycore, O.B.E.

Brig. Paycore is a forbidding figure who was the oldest of Uncle Adrian's chums. They had sailed together on the Yangtse, and kept sailing together over the years up to an Admiral's Cup season when both were old enough to know better. Brig. E. P. did not sail often owing to his advancing age, but would invariably find time for any trip which stopped for long enough abroad to stock up at a duty-free shop.

He acquired his stiff leg on the Somme offensive, not from a charge across the wire but following some communication difficulty with a Northumberland Fusilier. His distinguished Service career ended as O/C Mounted Regiments Fodder Supplies Indian Army. This experience enabled him to spend the five years after retirement as Chairman of the Central Midlands Gas Board.

He is now Commodore of the Brislingsea Yacht Club.

Major 'Sweaty' Knowles

Somewhere along the line Sweaty Knowles must have discovered something really nasty about Brig. Erstwhile Paycore or Adrian or both to get into the boat at all.

By his own efforts he turned a sizeable fortune left to him by his dad into a non-existent one. Gives the impression he was in a very posh regiment by mixing his Vs and Ws, and is Secretary of the Brislingsea Yacht Club. He also thinks himself as a walking Debrett of Sailing, an authority on the racing rules, sailing etiquette, and the social qualifications of any aspiring club member. Potentially he was a recipe for disaster, but by a stroke of good fortune Nigel caught him coming out of a house of very well known repute in Deauville, and the mere mention of that town within 500 miles of Mrs Knowles has been sufficient to maintain control ever since.

Nigel

I don't know what Nigel's other name is, but he must be the most faithful of Adrian's crew. We thought he did something in the City: he does, with a very profitable tea bar on Fenchurch Street Station. Nigel adores sailing, has been the butt of all *Lassitude* jokes for many years, can steer a good course when his glasses are not too salted up, and gets better on the fore-deck as the weather gets worse.

Raymond 'Nosey' Hawke

Nosey scratches a living as a yachting correspondent, and is quite good at it if he is reasonably sober when he writes the copy and then stays at about the same level to telephone it through. Sadly, many yachting events are reported by his paper by 'Owing to technical difficulties we will publish the Cowes results next week.' His performance as a navigator is about the same, but even with these lapses some form of Nosey is desirable in every boat as whatever his state he is a magnificent raconteur. When he can remember to go home, he lives with his mum in Basingstoke.

Letters to Creeper

Dear David,

I am pleased to hear that you got the boat back from St Malo. Next time you get stuck in fog off Selsey Bill run in on a safety bearing on the Nab Tower, the only time you will find the R.D.F. any use. I am sorry that Nosey Hawke did not turn up, he can be a bit unreliable.

Your letter suggests that you are worrying about sailing the boat: that is not the intention. The Arabian Oil Company give me more than I can drink; the idea of going sailing should be fun, doing it should be more fun.

You should be careful to avoid constipation. The movement of a boat has an effect on muscles which are trained to sit at a desk selling insurance of tightening them up when holding a balance against the sea, restraining the natural flow of things. On the other hand, the water and food taken ashore from all points southwest of Cherbourg has the opposite effect. A kind fate has therefore provided both the problem and the cure for yachtsmen on short cross-Channel voyages. What gets stopped on the trip to Normandy will get moved by a carafe of plonk and a *fruit-de-mer*. If the voyage does not fit in with this cycle there are pills which ease an excess of either ailment.

The more serious problem, however, is created by either process in that this change of habit with the additional cold, wet or dirt suffered in sailing will give you piles. These will make you miserable, and in turn you will make the crew miserable. Get them fixed next winter or take the harder remedy of living on a diet which is more cereal than gin.

Which reminds me that the only unpleasant job you have to do yourself is to unblock the loo when inevitably it becomes blocked. Claud Worth's galvanized bucket might have left its mark, but like the catheads of sailing ships or the high poop of a Chinese junk, was a practical answer to the problem. Since we decided to get decent we have to defy the hydraulic laws, and there have been more attempts to build a good marine loo than patents on nutcrackers.

They all leak, and block. An American friend came close to solving the problem with a notice which in its way made the point – 'Nothin' down here you ain't ate'. Whilst that was clever, he kept the old one too long, and it bust into a lot of pieces of porcelain. The crew didn't mind too much, but his wife who had been sitting on it when it bust in the middle of the Channel Race is said to have finished the race in a very low state of morale. With thirty more hours beating to windward she was lucky not to have suffered the most unlikely accident in the history of ocean racing.

I know your chemical contraption works at Chertsey. For God's sake don't put it in *Lassitude*, you will have enough trouble when you do a really good broach without having a downward-pointing chemical toilet. Leave the one you have got, put some new rubber washers on it, and keep it well swilled with that disinfectant supplied in plenty outside the hull.

Yours ever,
A.S.S.

P.S. Please tell Nigel I have his photographs.

P.P.S. You will be better off leaving Girl Friends ashore. At your age I do not expect you to take that advice. When they come to use the head do not expect them to understand the technology. Even if your mission in life were teaching Zambians to fly Concorde you will get beat on this one.

'Look Celia, first turn the big gate valve with the handle pointing forward, then put your hand under the stand and turn the valve on. When you have finished pump with the lever and control the flow with the little silver valve, then turn the gate valve off and the handle back pointing aft.'

If you try it, you will either have a tearful lady squeaking at you

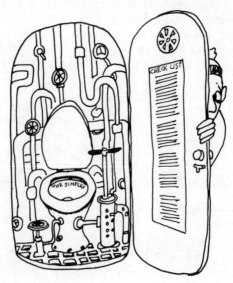

after half an hour that 'your loo' doesn't work, or worse she will come up with the little silver lever which came off in her hands. You will find it easier to bow to the inevitable at the outset and tell her to use the white thing up at the front and then ask Henry nicely to pump it all out when she has done her worst. If you must take them to sea for a long passage Henry will enjoy giving a protracted lesson before you start. It won't make any difference, but Henry enjoys that demonstration very much.

In either case never tell girls that in practical use the boat falling off a good wave will create a surge effect in the pan. That is a marine experience they are better left to discover themselves.

Yours, etc.

When told of the substance of Uncle's advice, the collected wits of *Lassitude* debated the finer points for some time. Their rather schoolboy jokes prompted by the subject were capped by a moderately sober Nosey Hawke.

'Your Uncle,' said Nosey, 'took us on an experimental cruise which I think was one of the first sail training races to Copenhagen. To make the crew legal he had the sons of several friends aboard whose wives have not, to my knowledge, talked to him since. After a longish passage we were bid to repair aboard the Royal Sailing Yacht for cocktails before availing ourselves of the shore facilities.

'Somewhere between the third and fourth gin and tonic the Skipper was overcome by a strong emotion which with a yacht in the middle of the harbour, and a Royal one at that, could only be satisfied by rushing below. As S.S. says, marine loos are badly designed and will accept but modest offerings, and for once in his life I believe the man was actually embarrassed when he found that he could not pump out what he had managed to pump in. With nothing to hand to beat it to death, Adrian came out of the hatch like a rabbit with a ferret at his vitals and gave up his chance to work for an O.B.E. for services to Yachting by leaping for the first shore-going boat.'

Cooking

One of the favourite shore time games of the crew of *Lassitude* had been to get their gallant Skipper into a corner of a bar, ring him in, and then bring on Rosie. Rosie was a heavy lass whose moustache glistened in her spectacles and who was supposed to have written a good book on Cordon Bleuing your way across the seas.

Having planted Rosie across the exit, they would then tend to fade away with a parting shot suggesting Rosie must tell him of the time she did that lemon meringue souffle in a Force 7 off the Sept Isles. The account was told wave by wave, white of egg by half pound of sugar, with the unsubtlest of hints that all *Lassitude* needed to really go that bit faster was a feeding programme for MEN.

The Skipper tried being rude: Rosie told him what an amusing man he was. He told her we were all vegetarians: she offered a mustachio nut casserole. He tried passing out: Rosie made a sporting try at mouth-to-mouth resuscitation.

Dear David,

COOKING

In harbour you should not feel unchivalrous to encourage any ladies to feed you, and be delighted if they can wrestle anything good from the limited cooking space in a yacht. At sea they will either make themselves ill in the process of cooking or become very very upset if you tack just when their beef bourguignon is coming to the boil. Also, cooks professing too much expertise will demand treatment and stowage space out of proportion to their value. You will find strings of onions round your binoculars, minced beef in the chain locker, and risk attracting the scorn of Sweaty Knowles and his ilk by getting a flutter of fresh vegetables falling out of your spinnaker when you break it out.

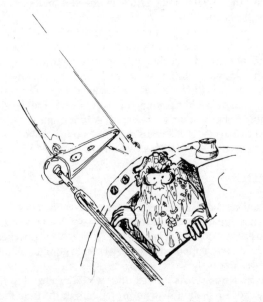

Hints for sea-cooks: a good stew is often spoiled by an unexpected tack.

The plain fact is that the heavy dose of fresh air laced with salt will make almost anything taste good, and the more there is of it the better it will taste. The two bacon sandwiches followed by an egg sandwich followed by a crispy bacon sandwich will taste better at dawn than anything your Diners Club card can command ashore.

As the most hardened tums will heave in the process of skinning a pound or so of kidneys in a seaway, supplies and menus should be planned on the principle of having the minimum time from packing to packing, i.e. tin to tum. This creates the minimum mess and seasick cooks. Sandwiches work quite well for short passages and are quite good fried when they start to become stale.

Meals should not be taken at shorebased times of convention but by whim of demand and opportunity, and if you get some cooking going on a downwind leg of a race, if it is short and sharp you will all get some calories aboard before the wind changes or you have to go round the next buoy. If instead you allow a couple of girls to wrongly think they can win your hearts, just as they add that pinch of paprika to the stew they were told about by Angy you will go round a buoy or broach and they will have added themselves to Angy's recipe on the cabin floor.

As tins are better stowed low, and their labels will sometimes wash off, you are likely to follow form by having at the end of the season a selection of slightly rusted tins without knowing if they are pilchards or stewed figs. To prove that your crew will not be fussed about the normal conventions or the order calories are hoisted in, give them a 'surprise' dinner, the rules being that they eat the tins in the order of being opened up.

On long passages, the reverse of instant cooking becomes true. Balmy sails across oceans will engender a laziness you cannot imagine, and the yacht and her crew will become intent in making great loops across the ocean rather than be bothered to gybe the headsails as the wind changes. In this environment, chess will become too much effort, the intention to read Shakespeare will not come off, and you will lose the better cards from the Monopoly set down the bilge. The importance of running a boat which has become soporific is to keep everyone awake so as not to hit the far side accidentally. The one thing in which you may raise a spark of interest is cooking, and one watch will try to outdo the other by turning corned beef hash into Boeuf a la Rissole de Sud Atlantique.

Providing they do not run you out of bottled gas too quickly and you have a good supply of milk of magnesia, this will do little harm.

Yours ever,

13

'That's right, quite right, quite right,' said Brig. Erstwhile Paycore, opening his mouth and pointing with a finger trailing off his tumbler, 'ook ere le ruddy toof I broke off.'

We waited with respect to hear the 'tooth' story.

'Yes, you see Adrian had spent this week with some girl over a bread shop in the Loire valley and thought he knew all about it.'

We waited with respect for the tooth story or possibly something better.

'Very funny it was boys, I'll have another whisky please.'

One was supplied through the hatch specially built into the boat for that purpose. Brig. E.P. gave every indication that the tale had finished and chuckled into his refreshed glass.

'You were telling us how you got your tooth broken in this bordello with the Skipper, Sir,' offered Nigel to keep the show moving.

The Brig.'s face changed from its usual speckled ruby tan to speckled vermilion. 'I certainly was not telling you anything of the sort. If you listened, what I said was that halfway across the Atlantic in '64 Adrian said he knew how to bake croissants. Actually they looked all right, what he had not disclosed was that he had had to bake them for four hours or something to get them brown.'

'So you broke your tooth trying to eat them,' prompted Nigel to get the story over and launch into his most recent Irish one.

'Good Lord, no, boy. You couldn't eat them, but they fell off the pilot berth as I was having a snooze after breakfast, the crash gave me that scar, broke my plate and the tooth.'

Nigel's story about the Irishman was too complicated to understand.

We did invite a Lieutenant (S) R.N. to sail a few weekends later, and disproved most of the stories about Naval Officers and Yachts, except that (S) must mean Sick not Supply, as he did one five miles off the Nab, and the other by producing his entire stores, a 14 lb tin of powdered egg and a 56 lb tin of red beetroot.

We tried this several ways without great success and were panting for food by the time we had tied up and run up Cowes High Street after the race. We drooled over the little glass case on the bar and asked for two crab sandwiches, four beef, two ham, four cheese, three egg and tomato.

The lady nodded sagely at each request and decided there were more than five items. 'I'll take for the beer first if you don't mind luv.'

Dear David,

PARKING

There is no way that you can learn to manoeuvre a boat. You find out by practice, preferably well away from the eyes of the curious yachting world. The two best bits of advice I can offer are:

14

Whatever time you leave a berth, whip off your lines and fenders immediately you are clear. It may be 0100 on a Sunday morning, but be assured that one of the Erstwhile Paycores of this world will be watching. The other gem is to know that for some strange reason of maritime accoustics no-one in a yacht with the motor running can hear each other, but observers from the shore will hear every word said in the boat for up to half a mile. Everyone aboard must therefore observe the discipline when manoeuvring of either saying nothing at all, or when remarks are made limit them to those which are intended for wider consumption. For instance, if you are just coming in after being thrashed on the racing course and caught several times running by Hartley-Smythe, it may make you feel better to pass a comment as you moor by shouting to the foredeck 'Are you sure Hartley-Smythe had that ballast tank fitted after he was rated?'

The foredeck won't hear a word of this, but your reward will come in the back bar of the pub later in the evening when you hear a suitably embellished version of the theme which will make a report in *Private Eye* sound like the *Dorking Advertiser*.

In parking there is a difficult balance to be made between observing the code of the yachtsman and finding somewhere to stop in the increasingly congested harbours. Getting where you want without creating offence requires some expertise.

Not surprisingly, the most sought-after place to park in any harbour is close to the conveniences – the club or the pub – and involving the shortest row to get to them. Such sites will be heavily guarded by other yachtsmen with large signs saying 'Reserved for members', 'No mooring alongside' or guarded in person by an unfriendly looking crowd in the cockpit of the boat you wish to lie

alongside who may convey 'Go away' messages either by glowers or by spoken non-invitations. 'Don't come on me old chap, I'm off in twenty minutes', or 'Sorry old boy, we've had to keep this slot for the Committee boat.'

In this type of circumstance it is fatal to ask Authority for parking directions, they will either send you four miles upriver to the visitors' mooring or tell you it is quite impossible and you'd best go back to Brixham. Nor is it wise to try to be clever and park in that part of the harbour which seems empty: it is a racing certainty that it will be for a good reason, and the good reason will probably show up at low tide. You have to brazen it out on the following ground rules.

Picking up somebody else's mooring is bad for the image of the conventional yachtsman and embarrassing if he comes back when you're all in the pub. However, if you observe the names of some of the better placed moorings as you pass the Harbour Master you can shout out '*Sunbeam of Lowestoft* is not coming back tonight is she?' If he says 'No, but you're not to moor there', rev up the engine, pretend you can't hear, and shout 'Thanks very much. Come over for your dues.'

When he comes alongside still muttering about the visitors' moorings up the river, finger your loose change until he capitulates and then pay him the exact amount for being such a miserable so-and-so.

If by some mischance *Sunbeam of Lowestoft* comes in, you can put your hand on your heart and tell them that the Harbour Master saw you in there and even had the cheek to charge you for the use of their moorings. How awfully sorry you are, have a drink, and seeing it's so late can we lay alongside for the night?

To go alongside a 'hostile' manned yacht between mooring buoys or piles, first put a good row of fenders out to declare war and approach the defender.

Defender: 'Don't come alongside please, we're off in twenty minutes.'

Attacker: 'Oh splendid, we'll stay on board to see you off.'

Defender: 'Did you hear what I said, Dammit?'

Attacker: 'Say, foredeck, what's that nice man in the super Hillyard saying?'

Defender: 'I said, don't come alongside.'

Attacker: 'Really can't hear you with all this noise. Have a chat when we're tied up.'

If you really think he is going in twenty minutes and don't believe it's worth the effort of establishing an armistice, you may as well reward his hospitality with phrases directed at your crew but loud enough to spoil his weekend. 'Cecil, be careful not to hold his guardrails. They look a bit rotten.' 'Say, Mike, are you sure you got all that tar off the fenders?' 'We'd better all get ashore right away or we won't get lunch. We'll probably get back in time to help this chap out from the muddle in an hour or so.' Or finally as you approach at a steep angle, 'I hope she goes astern this time.' If you play these in the right order there will be no need for further badinage. Chummy will retire to his saloon to sulk and be very nasty to his wife.

If he still has the nerve to drip, treat any argument as a self-destruct button. Look very grim, get up all your heavy warps, double head and stern lines to the post, breast lines to the boat inside him, drop the anchor 'in case the posts fall over', and go ashore for lunch.

On the other hand, if he is parked for the day and wants a clear view of the start line you may get 'Awfully sorry, David, but I'm keeping this slot for the Committee boat.' Don't tread on this one, he might be right. Try the 'Oh well, that's fine. If we lie here until they come. I've got to see Erstwhile Paycore about your summer cruise round to our lot. Couldn't be better. Thanks awfully.' He won't be pleased, but nobody will get nasty about it, and if you ask him over for a few quick drinks he will mellow as the afternoon progresses.

Static defence is indicated by a large board which says 'No mooring alongside. Reserved for A.B.C.Y.C. Members.' With this you have to wait until the Harbour Master has moved off out of sight, nip alongside, moor up and move his sign to the other side of his craft. When you've moored up, turn off the engine and from underneath the mattress of the starboard quarter berth bring up the sign which says 'Strictly reserved for members of the Royal Bruneii & Northern Celebes Yacht Club'.

Where you have to pick up a mooring at another club and are confronted with the club boatman, don't try 'May I use a mooring for the night?' He will tend to say 'No' like a G.P.O. answering machine. Do some quick research on the name of the club Secretary. Without wasting chatties tell him how nice it was for him to come out and meet us. 'Which mooring did (quote the name of the Secretary) tell you to put us on?'

Finally, and for emergencies only, the 'Yachtsman in distress' routine. This is necessary in absolutely sardine harbour conditions when you've foolishly arrived in the middle of Regatta Week. Having had a run around and absolutely despaired of slotting in any place, your only chance to stay anywhere other than outside the harbour will be to select the most inconvenient spot in the harbour (in front of the ferry stage, across the entrance, or under an open swing bridge) and then in what seems a panic arrange for the crew

*'Seems a good spot, George: I don't see why the Harbour
Master shouldn't let us stay . . . '*

to stop the engine and sling over a kedge anchor. In no time flat
you will be visited by the Harbour Master or his deputy in a state of
some excitement, and the conversation should then go thus:

Harbour Master: 'What in the name of Hades do you fancy
you're doing anchored there?'

You: 'Awfully sorry, Harbour Master. But the engine's gone
phut. Think it must be the injector.'

Harbour Master: 'It's no good. You can't stay there.'

You: 'Well I know, but I don't fancy trying to sail this ketch all
round your harbour.'

Harbour Master: 'For God's sake don't try that. Don't try and sail her out of there, sir. Here, give us a line. I'll tow you onto a berth.'

Q.E.D. for an extra pound you've made everyone happy. The Harbour Master has got an extra pound and a story which will keep him going for a month about this unbelievable twit who anchored under the swing bridge. You have a berth twenty-five yards from the landing stage.

Caution: don't try it in Salcombe. I did, and was given an unexpected and unwelcome tow halfway across Devon. There's a spot up the river there where two tides meet and the boat rolls twenty degrees all night. I am convinced that the Harbour Master reserves it specially for yachtsmen who try the 'yachtie in distress' on him.

If you are trying to select from a number of possible alongside moorings a certain amount of experience is advisable. When you are nearly out of booze, the boat with eight people standing in the cockpit at the stern of theirs holding full glasses could be a good choice, but you will have to balance the advantages this may have with the probability that you will have a disturbed night when the youngest, and drunkest, member of their crew comes back and tries to climb into your forepeak berth with either Nigel or a Labrador.

Potential rough nights are also indicated, and unwanted alarm calls certainly, by a boat flying a hoist of signals of four drying nappies or towing a small inflatable model boat or dangling a child's fishing line. However, look at such sights carefully before discarding them as you may have to weigh up whether you are not looking at an experienced yachtsman whose children have long since emigrated, but who is aware of the game and has carefully retained these 'lie here at your peril' signals to retain a peaceful outside berth.

Once you have tied up alongside there's a convention to cross over your neighbours' deck by first asking if you may, then walking across their foredeck and not across their stern. A fair exception to this is when you actually need a drink from the party going on in their stern, when you are more likely to get one nudging across the counter than by hopping over their bow. The other exception is to avoid crossing the foredeck of French club yachts at night. They will invariably come into harbour with twelve crew on deck, moor up, and then open a hatch and release another twelve who are off watch; the open hatch will also release a cloud of Gauloises and a waft of onion soup. The danger of walking over such a foredeck at night is that they may have a large open forehatch and falling down this may involve you in a very Gallic situation with two couples in the pipe cot below, or indeed to trip over a similar situation on the deck. Nigel fell down the forehatch of such a yacht the first day one Cowes Week and retained a glazed expression for several months.

No English yachtsman should ever try to emulate this, unless you first take the girls over to the French coast when you may be entitled to do as in Rome.

Yours ever

These pieces of wisdom were read to the traditional cockpit conference once the boat had snugly been tied to the trots with our 'No Mooring Alongside' sign to the outboard world. The sailing breeze had died to leave a calm and misty evening and prompted the story of how Adrian and *Lassitude* dabbled with the occult.

Uncle Adrian apparently had not been too keen on the story. With the aid of a failing wind and a strong west-going tide, and his navigational mate Raymond not anticipating either, they had on an early Volunteer Cup race to Cherbourg fallen short of the harbour and drifted on the tide to a point where an evening in Barfleur had seemed more attractive than a beat back to Cherbourg. They parked *Lassitude* against a wall and went ashore to have the best dinner their converted pounds could command, with a plan to leave on the next tide at what Adrian apparently described as 'O Gawd double O'.

After dinner a tactical decision was made as to whether it was worth sleeping before 0300 and the majority decision was taken that they would drink the remaining francs, which inevitably meant that they first used up the francs then cashed their remaining sterling travellers' cheques to keep them going with a half-hourly dose of Calvados.

Adrian got the crew aboard at about 0230 and they spent half an hour waiting to float off as the tide came up by making just enough noise to wake up the rest of the sleeping harbour, and indeed at that hour felt that this was justified as the calm and misty harbour was really quite an experience on such a still and magic night. One or two of the sleepers commented that they could not see these magic properties, but one way or another it seemed that they acquired a larger audience to the departure than might reasonably have been expected at Barfleur at 3 a.m. in the morning.

Without incident the lines, fenders and dinghy were imported and at a modest four knots Adrian headed for his estimate of the harbour entrance, which fortunately approximated to its static position. Somewhere towards the entrance somebody on the foredeck advised him that a sailing dinghy was coming towards him; Adrian didn't hear but Sweaty Knowles who did, and who had just finished rereading the *Hornblower Compendium*, shouted 'Ware away?' 'Out there on the right,' says the foredeck who hadn't even heard of C. S. Forester. 'Regardez-vous les bateau Anglais,' volunteered Sweaty Knowles. By the time Adrian saw the empty boat it was very close and still coming towards them quite quickly, and going hard to port and full astern didn't save it coming and giving them a hard thwack underneath the cap shrouds where a piece of French galvanized iron made a neat square hole in the topsides.

The effect on Adrian and the crew of being struck firmly and damaged by a completely empty day-sailing boat might have worried them on a fine summer's morning, but on a misty pre-dawn still harbour and on top of their recent plucky effort to drink the Cafe du Port out of Calvados, it was electric. A hesitant boatfull disentangled themselves and went back to the quay to inspect the damage.

An Irish coffee, more Irish than coffee, seemed to be the right mixture and though the damage did not seem to be severe the circumstances did, with the realization that even if the incident made a good story no-one would ever believe it.

The coffee revived their nerves and the yachtsman in pyjamas who had been reluctantly awakened to the evening's entertainment was looking down at them from the quay. 'Nasty crack you got there,' says Chummy. Sweaty Knowles was about to tell him the story of the Barfleur *Marie Celeste*, but the sense of normality alongside the quay made him hesitate. 'Strange, strange,' he mumbled as a compromise.

'Yes, typical bloody Frog,' says Chummy. 'Moors his dinghy up with half a mile of floating line. Funny, when I saw it yesterday I said to the wife, I said, that floating line, I said, very dangerous that draped all over the harbour, bound to get fouled in somebody's screw I said. And bless my soul the same night you get it right under your keel and drag the boat into you. Rotten luck I call it. Got any damage?'

'No,' says Uncle Adrian, disappearing down the hatch, 'fortunately we twigged straight away. I think we'd better get ourselves organized to get out of here. Goodnight.'

Dear David,

The conventions which govern going ashore arise from the rigid and efficient use of pulling boats in the iron men and oak ship Navy of a century or more ago. That background through the Navy has bequeathed to yachtsmen the duties of not standing on thwarts, shipping your oars with the wet blades away from your passengers' skirts, not standing up in the boat, keeping your fingers inboard, and allowing the senior officer to board last and leave first.

It is impossible to fulfil any of these niceties in a nine foot six rubber dinghy with a puncture in one compartment. Indeed, rubber dinghies do not fit the image of the grand yachtsman very well but are often the only possible form of transport and can be invaluable. It is therefore wise to follow Naval tradition in launches and hard bottom dinghies but to concentrate on survival in rubber ones. The only other convention is never to use another man's dinghy (however convenient it may be). You might also impose this convention on others by hiding your oars when you park it.

Before the marina at Cowes was floated we used to have to rough it at about a tenth of the cost in a mess of boats out on the trots. Half the fleet came for the racing, the other half as observers of a very distinguished Viscount who every year would paddle his Duchess Mum and Marchioness Auntie to the Squadron Ball. He wore the Squadron mess kit and the ladies long ball gowns complete with tiaras and sticks with silver tops.

I never believed that anyone reputedly so clever in Government would do this by mistake, so I have to assume that this exercise would be as close as a distinguished peer could come to attracting popular appeal, and as he was reputed to be no fool I believe he deliberately made this pilgrimage in a half-inflated dinghy. When he pushed with his feet it raised his body to pull on the paddles . . . and the middle of the boat would go up . . . the Duchess and Marchioness at each end would go down . . . on the return stroke his not inconsiderable bulk would go down on the rubber seat and Mum and Auntie would go up.

This fantastic seesaw would proceed rhythmically to the Squadron steps, watched by a large and spellbound congregation. There the boatman would fumble underwater for the bit of binder twine which served as a painter and the whole party would disembark, in strict seniority, and be saluted out of the boat by officers and men of the guardship.

Life now has more convenience and we have a marina, and a

launch service provided with a health warning on every boat. You may have more fun with your Brazilian bongo drummers; we were content with Blib, Blob and Also Ran.

Yours

Dear David,

COMMERCIAL HARBOURS

My letter about parking did not of course refer to commercial or fishing harbours. You will never see a fishing boat without a great string of rubber tyres down the side which are left there permanently except for the three days a year when they give the topsides a fresh coat of bright paint. In going alongside that boat in Brixham you were therefore lucky to get only paint on the fenders and that your bright career in insurance was not brought to an early end by an eight-pound piece of cod with a cross fisherman at the other end. The other snag about fishing harbours is that seagulls will support their adopted fishing fleet by trying to keep away yachtsmen with a heavy bombardment on visiting yachts, and while this will wash off your deck fairly easily it is not so easy to get off sails or sail covers. Whilst in general fishing ports will tolerate the odd visiting yacht, they do suffer from piles like commercial harbours and fishermen definitely work what the Ministry call unsocial hours. If you sneak alongside a working boat at midnight it may seem deserted, but at 2:15 the crew come down to work the tide and it can be an hour when you both may lack a sense of humour. You may be cast adrift in the harbour or taken some way towards the fishing ground before they let you go. In either case this will involve heavy fishing boots across the deck, which will sound like the Brigade of Guards keeping their feet warm on a cold morning as heard from the wrong side of a manhole cover.

Commercial harbours often have a lot of visual charm but decided snags, not least of which may be a distinctive smell.

There is no doubt that parking a container ship is harder if you have to warp it round a treble-banked line of yachtsmen who have 'just popped in for the night', and therefore commercial harbours are generally defended against yachtsmen first by a line of natural defences which are rows of thick piling outside the concrete wall, on which it is hard to lie without massacring your topsides. They then have a deposit of tar on the dock wall and a thick layer of oil on the dock which is likely to get trampled onto your deck. The other line of defence will be in the person of the Third Assistant Chief Dockyard Superintendent who will have a blue jacket, Post Office trousers, a flat hat and a yellow raincoat. His pay and function in life is so miserable that having the opportunity to put on his cycle clips and pedal round to tell a yachtsman to go away will actually be the best thing that has happened that day.

Third Assistant to the Deputy Dockyard Superintendent

Therefore, however beautiful a sunset or sunrise may be in a commercial port you are advised to stay clear except of the smaller harbours, and certainly to stay well clear of any ferry ports, where you will find a most aggressive reception, from traffic lights on the wall telling you you can't come in to a boat in the middle of the harbour telling you you shouldn't have come in, and a man on the dock telling you you can't stay there once you have got in.

Drying harbours create two problems when God pulls the plug out, neither of which are apparent when you go in on the top of the tide. The first is the position of the sewer outfall and the other is that the ground underneath you needs to be reasonably level and solid to hold you upright. The problem of staying upright against a wall has become an intellectual one and it has taxed the minds of many to devise schemes to keep the boat alongside and upright without having to stay awake all night to see her on and off the ground. It is amusing to watch some of these, as lines are taken from masts with blocks of concrete hanging from them on a single whip to keep tension on the main halyard, plus another weight on lines on the stern. However ingenious these arrangements, don't be too impressed. Heath Robinson down the road will still get up to see her 'on' and 'off', and if nothing else to make sure that his self-hanging device works.

Lying to a wall is not as nasty as it looks, and a yacht seldom falls over. The best tip is to have long drifts from the head and stern to the quay and to give your main halyard a good purchase to hold the boat alongside from the top of the mast. Nigel will show you an innocent ruse for mooring up whereby you put a clove hitch and two half turns on top of another boat's running slips when you are all moored in a complex situation to the same piles. This will stop other boats slipping alongside you and in the course of the season will greatly add to your stock of cordage.

Yours sincerely

Dear David,

Marinas

It would be nice to report that the impact of marinas had been totally ignored by the true yachtsman, but for very good reasons this has not happened. Whilst there was an initial disregard for these new-fangled moorings, the advantages of not having to roll up the yachting trousers and paddle half a mile in a partly deflated dinghy whilst the wife moans about the rain, the grocery box dissolves in the bottom of the boat, and your last five fags fall into the same puddle, are substantial. Only a handful of traditional Old

Gaffers and of course all the other yachtsmen who can't afford the £11 per week to keep a boat in a marina now debunk these very useful institutions.

Useful they may be, but should not be confused with anything to do with yachting. Firstly they mix in an arbitrary way the yachtsman with the caravan owner, a bit like having your club merge with the local association of the Old and Ancient Foresters without anyone asking you about it. Secondly the people who own marinas generally know a bit about making money, but not necessarily

much about yachting. It is therefore not surprising that a number give you the impression that you are in a cinema car park. The people employed to run these investments are almost invariably uninformed, and the job is awarded to some mariner based on the experience he gained on both the outward and homeward voyages as a utility steward in the tourist bar of a P. & O. migrant ship. However, with whatever background, the experience of being placed in charge of six hundred static yachts has the same powerful effect on them all.

Your Marina Master, as he will style himself, will soon convert his hut into a replica of the bridge of a supertanker. Large boards with magnetic clips, clipboards, high-powered binoculars, keyboards, halyards leading up to a signal station, a telephone and a met chart: this is of course all irrelevant to what in essence is a check-out point for a multi-storey car park, but his concentration on things nautical will mean that the hut will be locked at all times you want to telephone, collect your boat keys or do anything else useful. Private enterprise of going in yourself will be discouraged by an Alsatian dog who gives you an informed sort of look to the effect that he 'had' half the crew from *Battlecry* last week and you have no chance.

In theory this should not affect your lifestyle, but you should take care that the marina staff, drunk with the power of being able to dictate to so many boat owners, do not add you to their list of people to whom they give nautical advice. You will note that they will soon have a blackboard fixed outside their office and start giving gratuitous weather advice. This develops quickly into formal suggestions which result from these predictions.

'Oh, I wouldn't go across this weekend, David, been toying with the idea of putting up me South Cone.'

'Racing today? You must be joking. Won't be a breath when you get past the Needles.'

Make sure you have a good supply of fuel to motor across the Channel when they predict a hooligan and see that your reefing gear is working for the day of anticipated calm.

This uninformed advice will quickly spread and you will be helped to moor your boat and put your fenders back on the lifelines 'the way we like it in this marina'. The Marina Master will grow a beard and acquire a reefer jacket, a white roll-neck sweater and a small-wheeled bicycle. It will save you a lot of unnecessary effort or distress to not try to change this relationship. There is no way you will reach a position of respecting, or being respected, by your Marina Master. The best you can do is to live together in a relative state of armistice. The one gambit which could floor him is to take him off to sea. You stand no chance of achieving this as he knows perfectly well that his marine law is limited to the lengths of teak-planked cat walk and his days off will be rigidly committed to pro-pagating marrows at the side of his bungalow.

It will create little damage, so let him tie up the boat 'our way'. Let him tell you that a deep depression and a cold front are certain to wreck your weekend in Dinard. Let him keep a set of boat keys (not the ones that fit the boat – keep those in your sailing jacket). The state of total submission will please him immensely and he will speak highly of you when addressing more rebellious yachties. If the whole thing becomes insufferable, buy a large shoulder blade of lamb and distract his Alsatian for long enough with this meat to get in the hut and juxtapose about twenty of the little magnetic berth tallies on his marina berth plan. Marina Masters are not very clever and the whole of the next working week will be spent in using the yard launch to tow boats out of one mooring into another so that they comply with the plan. When you come down next weekend and see a troupe of non-seagoing yachtsmen pushing overladen trollies aimlessly round the pontoon to look for their boats . . . you will feel much better.

Yours etc.

Major Knowles had to add to the afflictions of marinas by mentioning the social difficulties of living in a large floating caravan park with neighbours who are chosen by whim of a magnetic tally and how you are likely to be inveigled aboard by your neighbour to hear stories of unbelievable nauti-cal balderdash. Their story of last year's voyage in a Westerly Pageant will acquire the aura of Joshua Slocum; their little woman will offer cups of tea and give the impression of putting up with this Outward Bound course which has been imposed by her husband so late in life as a cross bravely borne. While the huge floating motorboat when it has been taken to sea has frightened Father to death or made the rest of the family ill, and all would be much happier and have more spending money if they went off to a weekend chalet or caravan, but put up with the inconvenience of having a boat, and also *Lassitude* alongside, as giving a better social image.

While Sweaty Knowles made it seem a very unpleasant experience, it was clear from his description of Adrian's handling of their neighbours that there are ways of making the best of a bad job. Apparently, when approached by Mrs Next Door Uncle Adrian would feign deafness and without replying to any questions greatly uplift the lady's spirits by imply-ing she was really the owner's mistress.

From the large motorboat and family of static weekenders on the other side, Uncle Adrian seemed to have grasped that they were prepared to buy a taste of the salty sea from him so they could pass on some spirit of mari-time adventure at the tennis club on Wednesday evenings, and both parties acquired an unspoken pact which obtained 80 milligrams to the fluid ounce in return for ten minutes of potted yottie stories which may have been vaguely true up to 80 milligrams but between there and 120 could fairly be described as a string of unbelievable whoppers.

Dear David,

VISITING MARINAS

It is quite a different business visiting a marina to having a permanent mooring, and vaguely the same problem applies to pinching someone else's berth. You should not expect to be welcomed by the Marina Master, and if he cannot get down quickly enough to warn you off on arrival, just pick any old empty berth. Whichever one you select he will be down to tell you to move and to get across the 'We'll see who's master here' point of view at the outset. To save him too much enjoyment it is therefore wise to fit into the first slot. Don't tie up very carefully and wait for instructions, which will come as soon as he can puff his way on his mini-bike round the pontoon.

'Can't have you there, you know. C25 will be back this evening. Move on to G46.' If you had gone to G46 you would have instructions to go back to C25 by now. When you have got to G46 he will pedal round and explain that this is only a short-term arrangement and after five hours you will have to move again and that the minimum charge is 6p per foot. What of course saves a lot of his time and satisfaction is to slip in at dusk just after the day staff knock off and leave again before 0800. The night watchman will think that you belong there unless you give him reason to believe otherwise.

Marina owners will probably have a fairly grand house with three toilets in it for a family of four. When they build a marina for 600 boats their practical experience at home will lead them to build a lean-to hut with six toilets and three wash basins, or the same facilities propped up in a caravan at the back of the boatyard. On a busy day at peak periods this will mean each seat having to be used eighteen times in the hour and no organization, certainly not a marina one, can supply loo paper at that speed. It is therefore wise to use the loos at off-peak periods or, better still, walk past them to rather more comfortable facilities in a hotel in town, in both cases armed with a copy of the *Financial Times* or something more comfortable.

Yours etc.

From Uncle's letters it may be gathered that he had something of a complex about marinas, but he had in actual fact been a protagonist for them and an early debenture holder in one of the first marinas. The early marinas had such a command on the market of convenience that they had been able to fill them with a section of sailing society which almost pleased Sweaty Knowles. When he decided to move home and wanted to sell his debenture shares he found in the small print that he had first to offer them back to the yard and any premium on sale became theirs. As the value had gone up considerably he thought that this put their sense of humour rating up to at least 15-love and to even the score arranged a sale of the mooring to a very aggressive dealer in scrap metal.

Major Knowles was furious, but judging by the reception generally offered to *Lassitude* by Marina Masters, the war had been waged in depth for many years. As Brigadier Paycore put it, 'I wouldn't stop in that marina down in the West Country if I were you. They probably still remember the cheese.'

We poured him a drink and waited for the cheese story.

'Well, we were having a few days in the West Country, you see. Everywhere we parked in this marina they wanted us to move somewhere else or put fifteen West German boats outside us. As Adrian wanted to go out every day he was told this was very inconvenient and if he wanted to come to a marina he should *stay* there. Adrian accidentally knocked the Marina Master off the pontoon, had words with the 114th German to walk over the stern of his boat, and was then told by the management that he couldn't possibly leave until the visitors had gone the following Tuesday.

'The thing would probably have blown over if Adrian hadn't come back three sheets to the wind to find one of his guardrails had been pulled off, made a very bellicose row, and behaved rather badly by proving that the Marina Master was quite right and that he couldn't get out until all the alongside boats had gone. So he let them go and then went.'

'What about the cheese, Sir?'

'Oh yes, the cheese. Well, we had this couple of kilos of goat's cheese left from a trip to Brittany and Nigel stuck it under the manager's hut. Nigel has always sworn blind that the three of them in the hut spent the next month trying to get the others to have a scrub with Lifebuoy.'

Dear David,

MEDICAL

The subject of health in a yacht relates more often to trying not to inflict too much damage on the sailing body in the course of a weekend so that it needs more than a working week to recover. Quite rightly, the sport is conducive to having a quick sharpener followed by innumerable other quick sharpeners, to keep the spirits up and the malaria down. You will find some super-keen racing boats which pride themselves on being 'dry', but this means that they are either unwilling to carry that weight or that they are prepared to work harder at the problem when ashore.

After a bit of practice you will find that sailing hospitality will not make any difference to seasoned members of the crew or yourself. The danger is that the unaccustomed increase in the quantity will have a bad effect on younger members. At your age there is no way paternal advice will be heeded in suggesting they be modest. Just let them get on with it, but try recommending bars and clubs where you know the pressure from other yachtsmen fighting at the bar will make them wait for a reasonable time before refills. Strangely enough, some of my best racing results have been achieved with the crew suffering from unbelievable hangovers. You can tell this problem when you see boats' crews fumbling around the deck in pyjamas at the five minute gun. Whilst there is little you can do about it, certainly don't reserve sympathy for the afflicted, or start jamming the medicine chest full of patent remedies. If they are young and healthy fresh air and the excitement of a day's sailing will recover their health quickly enough.

The more serious ailments that can crop up in boats are not really treatable on short voyages, nor in a small boat is it really practical to arrange a burial at sea, even if you have got a prayer book. If you do get stuck or have a grisly bent to study things medical, there's a very good book aboard called *The Ship's Captain's*

Medical Guide. This wisely assumes your medical knowledge to be very limited, and that you will not understand any Latin words. It is basically laid out like a fault-finder chart in the same way as an owner's maintenance manual for a pre-war car, e.g. running roughly, difficult to start, follow column one – check distributor head, press in leads, check sparking plugs, and so forth. By a similar diagnosis you track down any sufferer and by asking suitable questions, follow through the course of the book and lead to some inane conclusion such as 'Nigel is pregnant!'

'Well, according to this you're about four months pregnant.'

It is wise to continue to stock a heavy pain killer acquired from the family G.P., and with these and some common sense you will have all you need for short voyages. The grisly prospect facing everyone is to have a serious accident. The best way to deal with really serious accidents is not to have them. Hands crushed in winches, booms dropped on heads, ties caught in flywheels, and legs crushed fending off other boats are best avoided by running the sort of boat where this doesn't happen. Without spoiling the enjoyment of sailing try to make the crew aware of the safety aspect, and your thinking and the first aid box should be oriented towards nasties. Of all the incidents likely to happen offshore, an accident is the one time that will make you feel you have got the better of a 2182 transmitter.

The prospect of having to operate for appendicitis on the saloon floor is remote, but the chance of dealing with a broken leg or a head that is bust open is not so remote. The ether aerosol spray which freezes both is a handy tool, but take care that having sprayed ether all over a gash you don't do a Sweaty Knowles and light your pipe and blow half the saloon to pieces.

The other endemic problem is seasickness. There are many who hanker after the notion that this is a case of mind over matter. You can only assume that these people have never been offshore in a foul cabin, cold and wet, with diesel oil in the bilge. There are circumstances where everyone gets sick. What you must avoid is to take people offshore who get chronically sick. Before you plan a trip to Brittany make sure that the people you are taking are reasonably stable closer to home. There are probably more accidents caused by excessive tiredness and chronic seasickness than for other reasons.

The only good thing about seasickness, and no-one who is suffering from it will believe you, is that the afflicted recover in a matter of minutes once inside a harbour. Their morale rises as quickly, and in no time they are explaining to all and sundry that they have not been seasick, it must have been something they ate. People also get used to going offshore quite quickly, and don't have to sail continuously in order to become immune or nearly immune. You can, of course, buy lots of pills to modify the effect but they all tend to

Offshore sympathy

make the taker sleepy and it's doubtful which is worse, having people full of sleeping pills dozing round the boat or having them sick. There are plenty of wrinkles offering prophylactics or cures, but the only real one is to stay at sea until the sickness stops, or stay ashore, but as chronic seasickness is so unpleasant people very seldom try the former. I personally reckon eating ginger biscuits helps. I don't think it has any medicinal value but I happen to like ginger biscuits and have a theory they make the boat go faster.

Yours, etc.

Nigel often gets asked for cups of tea by foreigners on Fenchurch Street Station and has therefore always been the linguist in *Lassitude*, and Uncle Adrian swore by him in foreign parts as he became completely lost when his efforts of shouting in a mixture of English, Cantonese and Arabic did not get the right results.

After a murderous social week at Cowes followed by a brisk sail to Cork, he and his crew were entertained for a week by the Royal Cork & Munster Yacht Club. This rightly thinks itself to be the oldest yacht club in the world, but being Irish their history is not precisely defined and they were not sure if their tricentenary came up in 1968, 1969 or 1970. An English club would have appointed a Committee to decide which year it was to be; an Irish club decided to celebrate all three years running.

The hospitality was immense and ranged from a bus tour round the countryside trying to find a typical Irish pub, which failed after the organizers had tried eighteen establishments and decided none were typical and went home to exercise the hounds, to a civic banquet at the Mansion House in Cobh, where the drink flowed free and speeches were made from the top table (standing on it) and replies were made from the floor, with the waiters dressed in Louis Quinze costume borrowed from a local repertory company whose lenders were either bigger or smaller than the waiters.

Even by Adrian's standards this was not a health farm. They then went on to Brest for a race which bad weather changed into a survival course. The culminating effect of a fortnight's singlehanded efforts to support brewery shares and a very lumpy ride round Ushant turned Uncle Adrian a funny colour, which any Pakistani doctor could have diagnosed. Nigel, however, decided he should look after his master and found a sympathetic French ear to whom he could explain the symptoms. After a very involved conversation he discovered that he was talking to a Notary Publique who thought he wanted to buy a plot of land near Quimper.

Nigel is not easily defeated, however, and after explaining the problem to the steward at the Club de Nautique de Brest a priest arrived. A further explanation ensued and Nigel acquired an address and a letter of introduction to the Clinique. Having collected Uncle Adrian in a taxi, Nigel took him to a large oak door and we're not sure whether the nun who opened the door or Nigel or Adrian were the most surprised. Uncle Adrian must have been poorly because Nigel and the taxi disappeared.

The crew never found out how the nuns managed to strip Adrian, but they got him into a wonderfully clean bed with starched sheets, gave him a sleeping draught and let him sleep till noon to let him recover from a fortnight's misbehaviour. Apparently it was not until he was shaved and dressed and was offering profuse thanks and payment that he realized that the series of anxious young men smoking Gauloises, the trolleys with new arrivals and the general scene of 'let Daddy have a look at diddums' indicated that Nigel had organized him into a maternity home. Nigel was told to go home by train but didn't and by the next morning even Adrian thought it was very funny.

My family doctor and his wife came sailing one weekend and I showed them Adrian's letter about medical health to ask whether if we published them in a book of letters they would in any way offend the Hippocratic Oath. There was slight wind and a hot day; we did a bit of ghosting and a bit of motoring and went to Poole, but neither the brandy nor a good dinner could revive the doctor and his wife from a severe case of sunstroke. As the doctor had said earlier in the morning, sunlight off the sea has the same powerful effect as sunlight off the Jungfrau glacier.

Dear David,

GOOD SEAMARITANS

Apart from mine, the worst source of unsolicited advice you will get will be from Good Seamaritans. This is a group of people who stand on docksides, in marinas, at the top of hards, and in general are freely willing to give you an unbelievable amount of cobblers about the weather, where to moor, how high the tide comes and what appears when it goes down, and should be avoided like the plague. Their advice will be either negative or wrong.

People who actually know about sailing will either be out doing it, or will keep quiet and enjoy watching you do it wrong. The true Seamaritan will be either the retired Sea Cadet arms drill instructor or some other form of land-based expert who would like to go to sea, but for some reason does not. They will watch you come alongside, try to catch your line but be hit by the thrown coil and drop the end in the water, which when finally caught will be tied by an unbelievable crochet knot to a wheelbarrow parked up the quayside. After lighting a pipe eight times they then tell you about the six yachts which were wrecked there last September. If one also volunteers the information that he is a fellow suffering yachtsman, find out if he bought his craft down the M5 on a trailer, and if so limit the advice you take from him to the quality of the cafes between there and Birmingham, and discard his advice about the yacht club, the port and its personnel.

You will do better acquiring local knowledge from a large scale chart, a sketch plan in the *Pilot*, and observation. Having started the conversation this type of Seamaritan is hard to dismiss – after all, his pleasure in life is to stand on the quay or the hard and bore you to tears. You will find over the chart table a small red French-Serbo Croat dictionary. Inside you will find some cards Nigel had printed which read:

THIS BOAT HAS BEEN CHARTERED
BY THE YUGOSLAV ADMIRAL'S CUP
TRAINING TEAM. PLEASE TO
TRANSLATE YOUR INSTRUCTION
TO SERBO-CROAT.

As you walk to the pub you hand the most dangerous looking Seamaritan both card and codebook, and will find after you have had two pints and lunch that he has gathered the whole advising industry in the harbour. They have made a plucky effort at translating 'You must not stay here, it will be dangerous as you are on top of some posts at low tide' first into French then to Serbo-Croat, and have drawn the local English Master from the comprehensive school into the argument. Some feeling is getting into the discussion with regard to the present subjunctive.

Collect the card and dictionary for use in some future haven, thank them in your best Serbo-Croat, and go off, as you intended, before the ebb starts.

Professional Seamaritans are harder to gauge, as you have to judge if they do not want you there at all, they do want you there if the bribe is sufficient, or they cannot stand yachtsmen at any price. As the bribe will be taken on any account, some commercial sense must be applied. If you think that you are tucked in properly and they are being difficult, a real or threatened appeal to the Harbour Master will usually call their bluff, unless it turns out that as well as running a mackerel boat he is the Harbour Master. As in other fields possession is nine parts of the law: getting tucked in should make you harder to shift than if you are warned off on approach. A determined yachtsman is harder to move after you have taken a couple of drinks from him.

Don't try it in Weymouth. Go to Church instead.

Yours sincerely

'Why doesn't the Serbo-Croat dictionary work in Weymouth, Nosey?'
Nosey explained. 'Commander Spindrift Smith was approached in Wey-

mouth by a very garrulous yachting type who was not only a good Sea-maritan but had a very fruity high-Anglican voice and was advertising his trade with a dog collar under his reefer jacket and yottin hat.

The Good Seamaritan

'Commander Spindrift Smith collected his card and dictionary and handed them to the Vicar with his best "I may not often go to Church, I break seven of the ten Commandments, but my heart is in the right place" smile. The vicar's face lit up when he read the card, and launched into a long explanation of why *Lassitude* should not stay there and take the ground on top of a sunken pontoon, all in presumably very competent Serbo-Croat.

'Adrian knew when he was beat, and steered the Vicar across the road for a "forgive my cheek" whisky at the Grotty Lobster. Over the second, third and fourth they discovered that they had made many common war-time chums around the Adriatic. Over the tenth and twelfth Adrian dis-covered it was either the Vicar's birthday or his, and shortly before closing time arranged a silver collection in the pub for "those in peril on the sea".

'Those in peril turned out to be the Vicar and his family, who would have been in peril had they gone off in their cruiser to Brittany without a new log. After their exertions in the pub they retired back to *Lassitude* for a nightcap. Halfway across the road the Vicar saw *Lassitude* where they had left her, but 10 ft below the quay.

'"Adrian, you old fool, I told you not to leave her there."

'"Gordon, you did nothing of the sort."

'"Of course I did when you came in."

'"Oh you really don't speak Serbo Croat."

'"Lovely." The two fell over each other laughing.'

Making a friend with higher connections was fortunate as *Lassitude* was balanced precariously on the top of a very rotten pontoon. Nigel had despaired of finding anything on the quay to fasten the main halyard to to stop her falling over, and had resorted to the rear bumper of a Ford Transit van, and was keeping vigil lest the van owner came back and drove off with an unexpectedly large tow of the top of *Lassitude*'s mast.

The Transit van turned out to be the Vicar's, and as both were safer where they were for the night, the two old Adriatic comrades were berthed in *Lassitude* and the alarm clock set to get one of them up in time for early Mass.

Dear David,

Colour Coding

The efficiency of all yachts either sail-changing or mooring can easily be judged by the inverse proportion of the amount of panic shouting and swearing.

When you have a full and practised crew the thing should work without further talk; when you have a crowd of girls and friends who are not used to the boat you will be wise to have a small conference in the cockpit before the evolution. Forget your knowledge of proper maritime terms and tell Cecil to deal with the blue rope pointing forwards, Daphne to hang the pretty blue balloons over

the left hand side about a foot below hers, and Bert to take the white rope under that rail at the back . . . tie it on first Bert . . . and fix it on roughly the same place on the boat we go alongside.

Like gybing a spinnaker, when everyone can get muddled between the old sheet and the new guys, you will find that what works is 'right, now pull the red one'.

Yours, etc.

P.S. Erstwhile Paycore is colour blind.

Dear David,

I note that this winter you are taking a course of instruction in the old *Cutty Sark*. I bet they don't tell you how she was sailed with ten men, four boys, cook, carpenter, two mates and a Master. I came round from Falmouth in her when she was bought by a training ship on the Thames; old mad-cap Steele let a cannon off for a salute leaving Falmouth and blew his whiskers off. Interesting Naval career that chap had, got into nearly as much trouble as me.

I think the Board of Trade or whatever they are now were pleased to be shot of yachtsmen, and I hope the Royal Yachting Association have got it right. They have been valiantly trying to justify their overdraft ever since by promoting the cry 'Educate not Legislate' and then trying to implement as many rules on the sport as they can. However, the principle is good and they are trying to stave off the evil day when this last freedom left to an Englishman – to go sailing – is not controlled by whim of wind or weather, or good or bad fortune, but from some department of the Min. of Ag. and Fish.

When you have finished your R.Y.A.-approved course don't be priggish about it. You will have added to a limited knowledge, in a limited way. They will teach you how to tie a double carrick bend (not how to untie that useless knot), how not to go aground on the Shingles or Shambles (not how to get off when you inevitably do so), how many fire extinguishers you should carry in a 29.6 ft gaff-rigged yawl (they will not tell you to watch the ones you have got to stop your crew finding the contents invaluable for some dry-cleaning process several months before they start a fire).

With your actuarial experience you will also quickly grasp the sums and be able to work out when a boat drawing five feet six can clear the drying bar off Yarm Head with a least depth of water of 0.5 blasted metres on August 14 the year before last. Don't try that one, use the sounder – English tides and winds have not been on the

39

course – and stick to what happens in practice where racing yachts leave when a retired Brigadier fires a gun, cruising yachts when the pubs close.

It might be a bit sad for people who aspire to sail to acquire all that theory first when finding out the hard way is so much fun. I suppose it might be useful for them to know you are joking if you tell them where to put their baggywrinkles, but it belies the truth that your actual average yachtsman spends

(a) 36.24 hours per annum sailing or motoring away from his mooring

(b) 111.94 hours per annum preparing to depart or arrive at state (a)

(c) 286.45 hours per annum purchasing equipment and discussing states (a) and (b)

(d) 2,174 hours per annum working to pay for states (a) (b) and (c).

When you have finished your course concentrate on my letters so that you look the part on or near your mooring, your friends bracket you with Robin Knox-Johnston, and most important so that you can realize that you do not know it all, but attract people to sail with you so that collectively you do. And that you maintain your status as the Master next to God and you can judge when they know what is right, but they do not find out what you know and what you are learning.

Yours, etc.

In the midwinter of my course, Brig. Erstwhile Paycore either very kindly or accidentally asked me to dine. When Mrs Paycore with the Brislingsea Bridge Club retired to exchange the really heavy girlie gossip, I learned of my Godfather's actual experience as an educationalist.

'With a file about a foot thick you would think the Admiralty would have known better, but some unbelievable twit posted Adrian as Officer Commanding a Pre-sea Officers' evaluation course in the Bahamas.'

'Not an awfully good example for the troops, really,' volunteered Major Knowles.

'Strangely enough,' said the Brig., 'that's almost word for word what the Court of Inquiry said.'

He unstoppered the port. 'No, the two things Adrian hated most were formal teaching and bunf, and I suppose he had crossed someone in the past who saw the chance to give him an overdose of both. He got rid of the teaching easily enough, and evaluated the leadership qualities by talking to candidates after the three mess nights he ran each week, and that worked well enough and proved as good a means of selection as any.'

'In the Indian Army we had . . . pass the port . . . Poonha . . . up from Rawalpindi to the area where these Pathans were giving a bit of trouble

. . . pass the port . . . but after poor old Archy Wavell went. . . .'

My bladder did not feel it would survive the reconstruction of Partition. 'Why did Uncle Adrian get carpeted, Sir?'

'You don't listen boy. I told you. Couldn't stand bunf. Stacked the whole shebang in an old barge, filing cabinets and all, towed it offshore and sank it. Replied to all letters for six months with a printed slip which said "It is regretted that all supply and executive papers of H.M.S. *Expedient* were lost on August 18 1945 by enemy action." Mind you it took another six months for the Admiralty to realize the European war had been over for months and the nearest hostile Nip was an undertipped waiter in Miami.'

Dear David

YOTTIGATION

This is an important subject and requires a lengthy letter.

Yottigation is an art – Navigation is a science. Owing to the violent motion, inability of yacht helmsmen to steer a course, and likelihood of large compass errors when the boat is heeled or has a kedge anchor parked alongside the binnacle, the science of coastal navigation is theoretically easy to learn but impossible to practice in a small boat. What is needed is the experience and art form of the Yottigator.

Sadly, no-one will ever be grateful to a Yottigator. If he brings the boat spot on the button to a buoy the far side of the Channel he will not be praised – the crew will quietly talk of the 'Jammy so-and-so' and congratulate each other on the good course they steered with the marginal adjustments they introduced to 'help him' during the two night watches. If the crew steered a wild course trying to hold a shy spinnaker all night and wandered between south and west in a poor attempt to steer 215°W, not finding the buoy will be entirely his fault.

Yottigators can only overcome this natural adversity by two gambits which introduce elements of doubt about the ability of the crew to steer a good course, the reliability of the compass, the amount of leeway the boat makes, etc. long before anyone is blaming anybody for a bad landfall. This is best done by having a sliderule and suddenly darting up to the cockpit, giving the helmsman a penetrating look and telling him he has been making good 240° for the last hour and what does he think he's steering (actually he's making a passably good job of steering 230°). The other trick is to sight across the compass and look at a setting sun or low star and come back after a flick through *Reed's Almanac* to announce that the port compass is reading 3° high, the starboard compass 4°

low – please take note, helmsman. Reverse this and in the logbook write '1816 Sun Azimuth port compass 3° low, starboard compass 4° high'. You can then produce the written evidence in your defence whilst floundering round the Cherbourg peninsular wondering if you can see Cap de la Hague or Barfleur.

If you are the navigator of a frigate, when you have checked the gyro compass to nil and ordered the coxswain to steer 235° the incidence of him going in some other direction is low owing to a long Naval tradition and the Queen's Regulations and Admiralty Instructions. In a yacht the factors which achieve that direction are far more uncertain:

235° on the compass may point to some other direction owing to a recently introduced and unknown deviation.

The helmsman may settle his myopic line of sight with a large angle of parallax on the compass card.

The spotty youth on the wheel thinks he knows that 220° would be a far more hopeful course to get to Alderney.

A sailing boat tending to come up into the wind will attract a helmsman above his course, and he will be pleased to think he is steering a good course by pulling the boat down to the right direction every five minutes or so.

Invariably four of these will apply at the same time in a sailing boat, and three in a motor boat.

Yottigation requires that you think of some arbitrary course in the general direction you wish to travel, and set the lads off to make the worst of that, and whilst feigning some other yottigation chore check with your handbearing compass the direction they actually achieve. You can then make adjustments to suit the various combinations of helmsman, personal feelings, failing eyesight and so on. Getting a boat organized down the same track as your theoretical pencil mark on your chart is the first, greatest and by far the most important factor of the true Yottigator.

If you achieve this and apply some of the simple rudiments of common navigation you will start to achieve a reputation as a wizard navigator, on the strength of finding France when and where you predicted. You can then start hamming it up a bit to generate a sort of mystique about the whole operation.

This is helped if you make some really lucky navigational breaks, like arriving in thick fog off the Morlaix River and then saying 'I think we are coming into Roscoff harbour' and without seeing the outer breakwater arrive in the inner harbour (don't try this unless you're fairly sure it is Roscoff). A particularly lucky break one summer when we were feeling our foggy way back from Brixham by Braille was to sail over the shallow patch a few miles east of the Eddystone. A non-Yottigator would have run up on deck and leapt up and down shouting 'I've found us' or something silly. A real Yottigator keeps this gem to himself, alters course to allow for the tide and just clear the western breakwater of Plymouth, and then wanders up on deck and starts rolling a set of dice. On the fifth roll you change course 5° and on the seventh roll change back 5° the other way. You then pick up the dice, put them back into the leather wallet, and as you go down the companionway tell the congregation that they will see the western arm of Plymouth breakwater on the starboard bow in about four and a half minutes. If at that stage you have been floundering about in the fog for sixteen hours no one will ever again challenge your expertise.

The danger is of nosey non-Yottigators trying to snoop at your charts and check your information. Don't make it easy for them: write as much irrelevant information on the chart as possible, leave your previous voyages unerased amidst a wealth of coffee stains and slightly plastic soaked paper so that they can see little of the printed word. If they ask, place your whole hand palm down, fingers outstretched on a chart of the English Channel and Western Approaches and say, 'We're about there, Cecil'.

They will persistently ask how long it is before you get there. A difficult question this. If you have a couple of birds aboard who are dying of seasickness the honest reply of 'about fifteen hours more' will be enough for them to reach for a handbag and take an overdose of Valium. Equally, a precise answer will not be easy if you have a very sketchy idea where you might be . . . hedge your bets. To the seasick always tell them another three-quarters of an hour. To the nosey crew make it complicated: 'Well, Cecil, if we keep going like this I suppose we might just take the tide off Alderney and make it by midnight, but it's too early to tell yet, Cecil. We'll have to wait and see if we can get the lift or not. Also depends on if you lot are making a decent course, ha ha, and we'll probably lose the wind west of the Casquettes.'

If you work out the tides that have affected your progress to date, and make good the course you intend, and keep a record of how far you travel, you will be as good a navigator as goes. The majority of apprentice Yottigators don't get those first essentials right, and then start getting frenetic with pieces of equipment to further confuse the issue.

The biggest confuser of Yottigators (unqualified) is one of the many forms of radio direction finder. Unbelievably, very few yottigators ever try to take R.D.F. bearings to test their accuracy when THEY KNOW WHERE THEY ARE. They wait to get the headphones out and start trying a bearing of Start Point when they feel they are probably somewhere in mid-Channel. Big ships with stable platforms, calibrated loop aerials and trained operators get absolutely rotten results from D.F. bearings. Yotties taking bearings alongside the engine block with a boat leaping about get even worse ones. Amazingly, however, because the set was expensive a greatly unfounded faith is applied to it, and having established a sort of null between 340° and 030° the Yotti gets his blackest pencil and draws a thick line down the 005° direction. He then does the same from the

'Lots of interference tonight, Brigadier . . . '

St Catherine's Point and Roche Douvre beacons. This gives him a cocked-hat triangle about the size of the county of Rutland and he estimates roughly where Oakham is, jams down a dot, puts a ring round it and pencils in the time.

It has very little to do with where he is . . . but he feels better about it.

Far more accurate guides to general position are the headings of a number of merchant ships travelling in the same direction, indicating the shipping lanes they are, or are meant to be, in; regular air flights, and cross-Channel steamers. An even better one is to hoist the two-letter code signal Church Pennant over Interrogative, indicating to the informed passer-by 'God where are we?' Or call up a merchant ship to ask for a position – if the ship answers in Panamanian, Greek or Taiwan Chinese tell them where THEY are.

In thick fog avoid asking people swimming or fishing off the beach for directions. Take the fact you can see them as an indication of shoal water: asking them if they know where the Clipper buoy or Ramsgate harbour is will merely elicit that they are strangers to those parts.

Yottigators need very little equipment but what they do need requires careful preparation. Their pencil, eraser and dividers will all attract unlikely uses for other people aboard, and should therefore be tethered on lengths of string like the cafe teaspoon. Dice, one set numbered, one set liar already mentioned, a set of charts suitably over-written and a *Pilot* book or two, an old copy of *Reed's* with a modern set of tide tables, and an A.A. book and railway timetable to add to the mystique. One item which is needed and also needs preservation is a pair of binoculars: these should be adjusted to your eyesight and then heavily boat taped in the right focus. Tell your friends this is to keep the water out. Actually it's to stop them using them when you most need them.

As a final wrinkle to Yottigators. Don't be fooled into thinking that what you actually see is the bit you expect (and want) to see. Check and doubt yourself.

One of those old Flying Boats came down in the China Sea when we were puffing our way up to Shanghai once. We were asked to look for some recently marinized R.A.F. types and set off in the general direction. As we got into the search area a speck was seen on the horizon. The pulse of the ship went faster and more and more goofers came up to the bridge, all with shiny binoculars acquired in Aden and little used since. The Chief Steward started the rot: 'I can see a tailplane.' The Chief Engineer then saw the engines, the Radio Operator saw the R.A.F. markings, the watchkeepers were getting a bit edgy about the whole thing because all they could see was a speck and were beginning to feel they would

'Sorry, mate – I'm a stranger here myself.'

fail their next Board of Trade eyesight test. The Second Steward saw some men standing on the wing, and the Purser someone waving a white towel. At about eight miles we were being treated by the gallery to descriptions of handlebar moustaches and wings on their tunics, and at four miles an apprentice unwisely stated that it looked more like a Korean fishing boat to him. At three and a half miles it clearly was a fishing boat, and at two miles it was a Korean one.

In the way of an unfair life the apprentice got absolute hell from everyone for weeks, but it only goes to show how easy it is to delude yourself into seeing what you expect to see. If you expect to see Barfleur lighthouse, make darned sure it is that before getting cocky about your landfall.

Chay Blythe and Robin Knox-Johnston plus eight million Australians can tell you of the funny light effects you can get where the Antarctic draft meets the hot Aussie airs of Wilson Promontory. This can sometimes cause the land to look upside down (confirming what many think about Australia anyway), and sometimes for images to split, two ships steaming at you, one the right way up and one sailing along on its funnel. All good stuff for curing alcoholics and amusing passengers after long voyages. What is very unusual is another ship coming at you down a line of mixed hot and cold air which splits the image. One big passenger ship sighted exactly that, two images alongside each other right ahead. The Navigator broadcast this interesting fact to the passengers who downed their drinks in a panic to run and see the most interesting outboard event since the Suez Canal. One Liberty Ship came down the port side, and the second one, steaming parallel to it, down the starboard.

With the exception of the Master, most observers were very impressed.

Two white lights and a green one above may look like a fishing trawler to you, and from where you think you are this makes good sense. The experienced Yottigator toys with the idea that this could also be a frontal view of Broadstairs High Street.

Yours etc.

Nosey Hawke was in practice a good navigator. Our navigational excitements occurred when he erred, by turning up on the wrong day, or not turning up on the right one. The alternative was a committee of the whole crew, which more or less worked once I had learned to trust none of them on their own at the science. The exception was Brig. Paycore, who could not navigate but had sailed enough to feel where we were when all else failed.

Sweaty Knowles fancied himself as a navigator and made myriads of detailed calculations and fine diagrams on the chart with his neat silver pencil. Tides were worked out, D.R. plotted, leeway applied and half-hourly positions reported. Any subsequent bearings or sightings would then be bent to comply with Sweaty's plot. If the chart according to Saint Knowles said we were off Guernsey, it was very hard to convince him that the bloody great lighthouse we were being swept past was Cap de la

Hague. His failing was not a hawk eye for detail, but an oversight of some of the basics. If it was possible to work out the tides for July 18 instead of August 18, not notice that the log read 987.6 before he started counting, or sound in metres and apply the reading to the chart written in fathoms, Sweaty would do it.

Nigel would not confuse the issue with charts or bearings, but would endeavour to throw all other predictions into doubt by observing that he had just seen a *French* seagull, or heard the BA927 flight to Amsterdam. He would try to convince us that Portland Bill looked like Dungeness, and could count the phase of any light in a way that made it look like the characteristic of a different and distant one.

You would think that, when he sailed, Wing Cdr. Trumpington-Jones would be *the* man, with his R.A.F. background. He had all the right cries, was very fond of the R.D.F., but practical experience revealed that his flying experience involved finding a set of railway lines which went in roughly the right direction until he saw a familiar gasholder. His working tolerance of twenty miles was a further limitation at sea.

While he could not help us get lost, it was Brig. Paycore who had the experience to find us again. It was he who would recognize the loom of a light where Selsey Bill was expected as being the floodlights of a home game at Portsmouth Football Club. It was he who knew that the Johnny Walker neon sign was a good lead into St Peter Port, and after a long fog in the Thames Estuary he who knew we were up at the top of the Black Deep.

'Knowles might be near the Tongue Lightship, haw haw, but the rest of us are up the Black Deep, haw haw, how about that Vasco de Gama Knowles, haw haw.'

A very frigid discussion was prompted by Sweaty on the theme that it was scientifically impossible for us to be anywhere else but off the Tongue tower.

'You can scientificate all night at me, Major Cabot, but yer water's the wrong colour for the Tongue.'

Knowles went through the theory for the fifth time, and added some personal nasty about Paycore's eyesight.

'I'd take a sounding if I were you, Magellan, haw haw.'

The fog cleared and we were alongside Black Deep No. 14 buoy. I asked the Brigadier how he knew.

'Couldn't you smell it, dear boy?'

'Smell what, Sir?'

'The sewage, boy – The G.L.C. liners don't discharge off the Kent coast – pump out here – Black Deep – easy, haw haw.'

Dear David,

Presumably because of the prefix, nearly all aspiring yot navigators become very excited about the word Sextant.

Classes all over the country teaching Yot navigation are full of people (either Yotties or 'couldn't get into the pottery or yoga class') unravelling the mystery of Marc St Hilair (a very interesting American who got lost off the Bishop Rock) and learning about GHA and traverse tables. All good cries, but the enthusiasm is out of all perspective – few of them have yet mastered the more practical art of the run from Newhaven to Calais.

Concentrate on this, leave the study of the stars until you have time, i.e. when you are four days out of Falmouth.

If your Atlantic crossing does not mature, sextants make very good bases for reading lights.

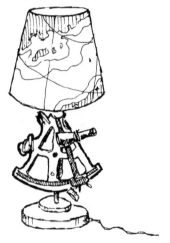

The best use for a sextant

Dear David,

YOTTIMET

This is the study and application of information supplied by a kindly Government service, the Meteorological Office. Basic non-Yotti information can be obtained about this subject from many textbooks. Totally disregard advice from Marina Masters, longshoremen, your mother-in-law, seaweed on the door, and bunions.

49

Even *Reed's Almanac* transgresses the borders of science by including poems which link the colour of the sky at sunset with the aspirations of a sailor. Seeing the editor-in-chief of *Reed's* is very definitely a yotti, and a seaman, it is surprising he has allowed this lapse. If you tried telling any old salt that a red sky at night is likely to be his 'delight', he would think you a sex maniac to associate the two.

Stick to the information gleaned from the newspaper, the radio and your barometer. In addition to the standard knowledge and equipment true Yottimet needs two pieces of special equipment.

Alarm Clock   This is vital and should be set to ring just before the shipping and other forecasts you wish to hear. If you don't have one you can go for weeks waking up or remembering to turn on the radio just as the forecast ends and the nice gent at Broadcasting House says 'We now rejoin Radio 4 for the cricket scores/farming news' or whatever comes after the forecast. (If you just miss the forecast but the BBC gent says 'That is the end of the Shipping Forecast. Good sailing and good luck gentlemen', either stay at home or head for yours or somebody else's quickly.)

Meteorological Office Golf Club Fixture List   Met men do not go sailing (they know the weather is too unpredictable): they play golf, and can generally read the portents well enough not to be caught out too far from the clubhouse in a heavy load of 'precipitation'.

You may have been conditioned by the publicity department of the Met Office and kindly television 'forecasters' into thinking that Meteorology is now a highly organized, accurate and computer reinforced science. So it is: the computer predicts accurately what is likely to happen from the last available information of some satellite or selected weathership report. It still requires human interpretation and is quite correctly called a forecast. So, if you recall, is the name given to your effort with the football pools week by week in the winter.

On weeks for 'away' fixtures of the Golf Club, the senior Met men organize an apprentice Mettie for duty whilst they travel by coach to Argyll. The apprentice is given a number of highly sophisticated options predicted by the computer together with the office set of poker dice. Four jacks and a ten . . . Humber Thames Dover . . . Light variable. Full house . . . queens on tens . . . Wight Portland Plymouth . . . south west decreasing later . . . and so forth.

This works quite well, and nobody can tell the difference except for the rare occasion when a low pressure system has crept in under the eyes of the satellite and is tailing a bigger system and creaming up the Channel at fifty knots. The apprentice Mettie is still churning out low throws like three nines when to his alarm Coastal

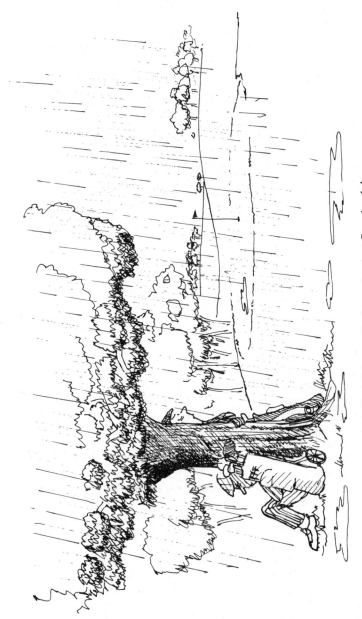

A case of a full house (jacks on tens) at Sunningdale

51

Reports and ships from the Western Approaches start giving him the tip that he should be up to at least four kings. He then has to wait for a respectable hour to telephone the Ancient Argyll Golf & Curling Club to tell the Club Captain that something is definitely not three nines off Penzance. The boss then takes a hand with Fate and tells him to update the forecast to at least five queens in Plymouth Wight Portland, four kings and an ace on the rest of South Coast, and three jacks and two queens backing to five queens with heavy rain later for the East Coast.

You can tell these away fixture weekends without a fixture list when something nasty happens which is predicted twelve hours after you had it. It is, however, prudent to be expecting the unexpected.

All weekends with home fixtures will give you very good forecasts. You may not get it quite when they say . . . but you will get it.

Yours, etc.

Dear David,

YOTTINGINEERING

The two aspects of marine engines which most affect boats are: (1) Companies who build marine engines are sited deep in dry farming country or well away from nasty salt water in the heart of the industrial Midlands. The official reasons for this are their need to concentrate on their main line of trade to make truck or tractor engines. The real reason is so that they can remain aloof from the concept that their product will start becoming rusty at its first brush with salt air, and that the process will continue on subsequent meetings. The owners will spend the next twenty years trying to keep this at bay. (2) Designers and builders who plan or build marine engines into yachts have a masochistic wish to place them in the most incredibly difficult places: if they can, at the back of a slot between two bulkheads under the cockpit or in an impossibly difficult space under the floor of the saloon. Indeed, if you go into a production boatyard you will see that operation one is to pull the fibreglass hull out of the mould; operation two is to put the engine into this vast open space; and operations three to twenty-six to build bulkheads, lockers and a lid all round the engine making any subsequent work on it a feat worthy of a limbo dancer or a small animal able to put 25 ft-lbs on a torque wrench.

However, once in the boat marine engines have to start swaying about and adjusting to their surroundings. Anyone who knows

Rudyard Kipling's poem about a new ship where the various parts have to live with each other's stresses will understand that the thing has to 'tune' in, and marine engines will acquire an individual Character (note the capital C). It is this which the Yottingineer needs to understand.

The manual for the engine will say, for instance:

> 'Changing the filter is a simple operation; remove the retaining nut at the top, drop down the filter bowl, change the XYZ cartridge and replace taking care to see the retaining gasket is properly seated.'

To do this in your boat means taking up the cockpit floor, and then finding you cannot squeeze down the hole – in desperation you hire the small boy from the boat on the outboard end of the trot. Give him a Coke and lower him down the hole with simple instructions. The wing nut on the top does not give up easily, but after you have adjusted the Mole Grips several times he gets it loose and takes off the filter without difficulty.

An accessible engine

Unfortunately he drops the wing nut down the sump. You spend half an hour fishing from the front of the engine with a magnet tied to a stick trying to retrieve it, before the helpful neighbour tells you that that is the only non-ferrous part of these particular engines. You charm your slim helper with promises of funds for the fun fair to keep him down the hole trying spare nuts you have in the tool kit. After another half hour your friendly neighbour comes back to tell you that those engines are all Universal threads . . . you have a selection of Whitworth and metric. You bodge the whole thing up with boat tape for that weekend, and the boatyard charges you £27.30 to fit a new filter unit. When this sort of thing doesn't happen you are becoming in sympathy with the Character of your engine.

I was 'larned' of the vagaries of marine engineering by one Bertie Woolstock – fisherman, inshore, East Coast. He ran an ex-Admiralty something or other in which he had a converted Buick car engine. The conversion had been basic, but logical, as he kept the back axle assembly and rear wheels on the engine to work a winch for the fishing gear. When this ensemble did not perform to Bertie's satisfaction he took out the plugs one by one, held them at arm's length . . . and spat on the points (in a moving boat not an inconsiderable engineering feat). When the plugs were replaced the engine would roar off into harmony except when Bertie tried taking off more than one lead at a time. He would then most likely put some back out of order. This meant he had to repeat the spitting routine, and on the second shot would get the plug leads in the right firing order. This proved, to Bertie at least, that the treatment worked.

Now you will not find gems like that in a maintenance manual – but it works, or it did for Bertie for thirty years. You may not think that the technique is mechanically sound . . . maybe not . . . but Bertie's engine knew that this personal treatment meant that Bertie 'cared' for it. The engine never went for anyone else after they put Bertie 'away' (not that he went mental, he had been that way for a long while – it was just that when the National Health Service got itself organized the general standards of normality moved away from Bertie's).

My other useful experience was trips with a favourite Uncle who kept a decidedly non-Yottie vessel for fishing in the summer and wildfowling in the winter. Neither his farming life, nor the purposes for which he had a boat, nor for that matter his notions of Yottin would seem to have any connection with this theme. He was, however, a great Yotti and had kept up a strong interest, and had a good library of all that was best in nineteenth century sailing. He had not greatly troubled about or become interested in anything that happened thereafter.

One notion he held strongly was a tip he had from Joshua Slocum about the danger some of these newfangled paints could do to good timber. As he was unable to obtain any proper paint after the First World War and they closed the town gas works so he could no longer buy tar, he had thereafter to let the bare timber take its chance with nature. He also had a theory about ballast, where his perfectly stable fishing boat needed some weight 'to keep it steady' (it certainly made it sink more quickly).

When he had come to ballasting his boat he had inquired the cost of pig iron and been horrified to find this more than treble the price he got for selling farmyard scrap. To avoid the expensive re-smelting process his boat was ballasted with a fantastic array of tractor hubs, an anvil, the more solid iron parts of an obsolete threshing machine, and the cross beam of a drill.

The engine that propelled this floating agricultural machinery museum was called a Fowler diesel. It must have been a good-un because his Uncle had it in a tractor for years before it was 'converted'. The starting was the good bit where you heated up an iron bar with a blowlamp and when red hot screwed it into one of the two cylinders to get its heart started. The pot which received this offering had a slightly longer stroke than the other.

Against his better instincts Uncle was persuaded to have the engine serviced one year his peas did well. The young marine engineers took it to pieces and had many good pints on the story that the long piston was in the short pot and vice versa. . . . Having had their giggle, they gave the matter some thought, a process which requires puffing the traditional marine engineer Woodbine soaked in diesel oil, and put it together again in an order close to the original design state.

What they had missed was the basic Yottingineering understanding about the Character of an engine. After forty years the engine, bearers, shaft and the boat that carried it had got used to having one great THWACK from the high-compression cylinder followed five seconds later by a modest little PUMPH from the low-compression partner. Put back together, the noise sounded musical to the mechanics. Uncle listened, doubted, and told them 'Don't seem to have the right sort of sound to me.'

Uncle was right. The unaccustomed regular vibration wrought havoc. The engine bearers went wobbly, the shaft log wore out, and worse the starting did not like the new regime. He was a kindly man and did not want to offend the mechanics, so put up with the problem and developed a new starting technique which did work. This was to soak a bunch of cotton waste tied to a stick in diesel oil, light it and heat up the general head of the engine and air inlet. (Somebody had given him a tin of ether to spray in, but he felt the aerosol was a little too akin to a ladies' hair salon, and also his adviser had forgotten to tell him not to attempt both systems at once . . . trying this had caused a two-bucket fire instead of the normal starting operation which could be dealt with by half a bucket.)

There was no doubt whether Uncle was very pleased when the engine took a hand in this new and undesirable state, and pushed its way through the garboard strake, through which a couple of tides slipped and necessitated the second major overhaul in forty years. This time there was no compromise and the pistons went back like they were originally.

Hey presto, immediate return to the satisfying THWACK . . . PUMPH . . . THWACK . . . PUMPH . . . THWACK . . . PUMPH.

Encroaching age had obliged Uncle to give up fishing, and some years later I was doing some off Scarborough one very foggy summer afternoon when I heard the familiar alternative octave sound. Out of the mist came the old boat, heavily painted in bright colours and fishing again commercially. Suddenly I could understand what Uncle had seen and known for so long. On every THWACK stroke the upright exhaust pipe blew a perfect smoke ring; the PUMP stroke was less vicious and wafted the rings away without spoiling the symmetry. Any engine that can do that both has style and must be running right.

The moral of these tales is that you must learn to live with the limitations of your engine and they with you. When in harbour at a still berth you can do what you like according to the manual or your own inclination. Change filters, run around with a dipstick looking for a dirty rag, and fill up the stern gland with the blackest grease made. My general advice is to do less rather than more on account of the exorbitant cost of hiring expert help to put it all back together in the right order.

However, at sea you MUST HAVE THE MEASURE OF THE CHARACTER of your engine. See it is receiving a regular supply of good clean fuel and that the water supplied mixed with diesel by the marina tank is drained off. Also that its guts are given the advised amount of oil; run it at a speed where you can feel it is happy. See that the battery is fed with a good supply of nimble Amps. If it is uncharitable enough to do a nasty on you offshore there is no way you can do an engine overhaul down the end of an obstacle course with everything leaping about. You are restricted to a limited procedure, having checked that you aren't out of fuel, of getting diesel spraying through the injectors, which may mean bleeding off the drop of water or air bubble you are trying to run the engine on.

If that doesn't work, Marshall's *Seamanship* Vol. II, Chapter 16, 'How to Berth Ships Under Sail'. If you are not on a sailing ship *Reed's* section on salvage and towing will serve.

Yours, etc.

Dear David,

FLAGS AND SIGNALS

Nothing shows up the uninitiated more surely than ignorance of the very rigid rules of the sea. Not the 'Red to Red, Green to Green, perfect safety if you're seen' variety, but the 'Good heavens, Erstwhile Paycore, just look at that fellow Trumpington-Jones going awf with his fenders danglin', or 'Here, Knowles, go over and tell that fool Creeper that the way he's dressed overall spells something unprintable in International Code and his blasted courtesy flag's upside down on the inferior yardarm.'

Sounds all very complicated but isn't:

Flags First You need a Snotti Yotti flag at the back – anything other than a Red Ensign requires some endeavour. A white, blue, plain or defaced ensign needs two chits of paper, one showing the 'ship' (albeit a twenty foot plastic sloop) as British registered. A process of form-filling between you and the Customs House from the port at which you register, plus a diversion thrown in by a Welsh lady from the Registrar of Shipping and Seamen, Llantrisant Road, Llandaff, Cardiff – I'm not joking – who tells you about 16,000 names you CAN'T use. When you have exhausted the bureaucracy and obtained this magnificent blue 'Registration Book' you then obtain through the Secretary of your Yotti Club permission from the Ministry of Defence to 'wear' the ensign. Don't sound too enthusiastic to get the warrant – play it on the 'Registered the old lady, as it comes in handy cruising south of Brittany. Stick in a warrant for me, old chap, so I can fall into line for our Regatta Week.'

Don't dream of not bothering.

Whatever ensign you achieve, only have it flapping on the back from sunset to sunrise, or when other Snotties take theirs down, or when you are on the move at night.

The ensign should be complemented with a triangular flag (or burgee to give it its Snotti title) at the masthead; i.e. if you are showing the Royal Brunei & Northern Celebes ensign you should have the R.B. & N.C.Y.C. burgee.

If you are, or are pretending to be, racing put a square flag at the masthead and take your ensign off.

The other flags you need are national flags to hang up on the starboard side of the mast when visiting foreign parts – preferably the same flag as the country you're in, and a yellow one to indicate to H.M. Customs that you have come back to dear old Blighty and wish that they repair on board, make everyone feel they are guilty of something, and, if time permits and you look a bit shifty about the extra half bottle you tucked under the sump, pull the boat to pieces and in all cases now give you the feeling that somewhere on passage you acquired a pack of rabid foxhounds.

Trying out other flags can lead to trouble, and you either need to stick at three or buy the lot plus *International Code of Signals* Vol. I and Jack Broome's *Let's Make a Signal*.

Don't try to be different – one racing boat I bought second hand from a very distinguished owner. A cleanout of the bilges produced a most exotic racing flag. Inquiries round the bar were unable to place it and we decided to fly it on the supposition that someone would be bound to trip on board with a 'Fancy there being another racing man from the Manchester Union of Oddfellows' or 'My word, old chap – C.I.A. Sailing Club, what.'

Truth was, we had somehow acquired a flag with the Logo of a well known egg producer. This was recognized by a sharp-eyed lady and resulted in a rather pert letter from her Snotti husband about 'the undesirability of introducing advertising into Yottin.'

Dipping Ensigns Not really a Yotti custom – just fun once a season to try on a passing Coastal Minesweeper to watch the resulting confusion spread downward and aft of the bridge.

Signalling by Semaphore Forget it: any knowledge of the subject smacks of an unhealthy association with boy scouts and nobody can read it these days even if you can send it.

Signalling by Light A difficult skill to acquire short of going to classes run by a retired C.P.O. bunting tosser who can trot out messages by the hour which say 'Fresh water can be obtained 20 paces N.W. of the landing stage' and when written down by your fellow sufferer (Morse is more fun in pairs) reads back 'Freshwater Bay is mined something something dammit by the Fangind Stade'. If you are going to be a lazy Snotti it is better to remember that W indicates that the sender's light is badly trained – i.e. imply that it is *his* fault you can't read it. This will shut up and confuse everyone bar Warships – they have the means and manpower to send a boat over with a courteous note if they feel that strongly about it. If you happen to be sailing across their firing range or in a path where they fancy launching a Phantom the same applies, and it's good initiative training for them not to let their war games go quite to schedule.

Signalling by Radio   There are a hundred ship-to-shore radios in yachts to every yachtsman who knows how to use one. For this reason you have only to say 'British yacht *Sea Urchin*' three times to put up the blood pressure of a number of normally patient coastal radio station operators by ten points. Yotties can therefore expect neither courtesy or precedence on the air. According to the instructions you should be able to chat to your office with your five watt transmitter from the other side of the North Sea. In practice you will find the competition from commercial traffic makes it very hard to raise North Foreland when you are off Margate Pier. Nice things to have, though, and you will get the cricket score on most of them. If you really want to talk round Europe (and have a few nosey eavesdroppers), you'd better trade up-market in output and add a correspondingly large bank of batteries or, far cheaper, telephone from the nearest pub.

Yours sincerely

'Calling Lima-Alpha-Delta-Bravo-Romeo-Oscar-Kilo-Echo-Sierra. A Tenner each way on Slowcoach for the 4:30 at Goodwood. Over and out.'

This prompted a signal story from Nosey Hawkes.

'Adrian somehow got us into the middle of a horrendous Naval exercise in Lyme Bay one night. Submarines, minesweepers, frigates dashing about, aircraft carriers flying off planes, and all without lights. After several incidents of vessels flashing past in the night we had tried shining the Aldis, hoisting the radar reflector, turning East, and hands to prayers, and we really were getting fragile about the whole question of the Defence Estimates when from about fifty yards on the starboard side a whopping

59

searchlight was turned on us from a darkened ship of that big sort that started as cruisers, converted into aircraft carriers, changed to commando ships, and back to cruisers with a big box on the back.

'"What Ship?" flashed the light. (Bloody cheek to assume a yacht could read Morse).

'"*Badly Shaken* of Hamble," we said.

'"You are in Exercise Bloodnot. Clear the area."

'"Which way at 4½ knots?" Pause for thinking by Officer of the Watch.

'"Suggest sinking where you are."

'The Navy like to have their little funnies with signal lights. But that particular time we did have the last word.

'"B-A-N-G B-A-N-G Y-O-U-R-E D-E-A-D," flashed Adrian.

'As they increased to twenty-four knots they just missed us with their stern, but it took several stiff tots to settle down. A further few stiff tots made us quite enjoy the free show and we were desperately trying to sort out the next exchange of signals which we wanted to send in Russian, e.g. "Hullo Comrade Jack." "Lovely fishing place here." "Force Blue has just torpedoed your carrier." "Love from Captain Pechiva."

'By the time we had a loose translation ready, we had made a bit of easting, and the fun fair a bit of westing, and when we tried it out we did not seem to be getting the rise we wanted. The signalling became a bit confused so we started again with the international "What Ship?" routine.

'"Trawler *Petrograd*, U.S.S.R."'

Dear David,

Social Sailing

Thank you for your letter about crew uniforms for this summer. I do not object to the expense, providing you think the boat will go faster dressed uniformly in Nipple Pink, but believe you will have difficulty in making a silk purse out of your sow's crew. Nigel will not work the foredeck in anything bar his Wimpey donkey jacket, and Nosey tries hard to do his navigating inside the doghouse and away from anything as nasty as salt water. The idea that Paycore or Knowles would conform to any new trend over their oilies patched with Avon dinghy repair kits is as far fetched as a Zionist peace conference in Mecca.

Sailing is a social sport, and you have to draw a line between behaviour that Sweaty Knowles would like imposed on the masses, whereby sailing is limited to the same set who get tickets for the Enclosure at Ascot, and whose crews make those on the Royal Yacht look dowdy, to the other extreme where a crew go into a yacht club and act and dress in a way which offends the establishment. Before this sounds like a Victorian book of etiquette you should also note that I have misbehaved for a generation in this sport and it is only important to know how to do so within the conventions.

A few years back the *Daily Mail* were trying to muscle in on the monopoly of reported sailing held by the proprietors and cartoonist of the *Daily Express*. A very good looking woman of the former suggested I write them an article about sailing clothing when she was seeking and obtaining some background atmosphere in the back bar of the Gloucester. For reasons unconnected with the fee, or my wish to become a yachting writer, I created for her an authoritative masterpiece about sailing clothes. Had she told me at the outset that she could not stand close proximity to short beards, and that the purpose of the screed was to be editorial support for a sales campaign of some bright plastic oilskins to their uncovered sailing public, I would not have bothered. Especially as it was called 'Mail Gear'.

The journey of anticipation is often better than arriving, and I enclose a carbon copy of the offending article which tells you all you need to know about sailing dress.

Yours ever

Dearest Sweetypie,

As arranged last weekend I have written down the salient points about yachtsmen's clothing, but having no claim on literary style I believe you could greatly improve the form and suggest you do so on a short trip I think I could arrange in my boat *Lassitude*. Next week would be fine.

Yours,
Bristles

Yachting Clothes

by Cdr. A. Spindrift-Smith, D.S.C., R.D., R.N.

Dressed in his well pressed Marks & Spencer pants and clean white Raelbrook shirt, our village postman once made a very shrewd remark. From his vantage point outside the Batsman he observed the Squire trimming the privet hedge outside Manor Lodge. The Squire was kitted out in his demob flannels patched with gingham to port, red and white spotted to starboard, and leather patch astern, a large houndstooth shirt with white inlets lengthening the sleeves, and capped with a fedora his wife had discarded when she decided she was no longer a Flapper.

'You know,' said Bates, 'You 'as to be bleedin' rich to dress as bad as the Squire.'

This piece of wisdom has not escaped the true Yachtsman. You must dress to the convention but never, never look smart. One or two who have tried to upgrade the Yotti image have been ostracized – one noted South Coast yachtsman who dressed with a clean Harry Belafonte shirt and matching vertically striped flared trousers one Cowes Week has ever since been known as 'Danny la Rue of the Solent'.

The folk who sell yachting clothes have been blowing rhubarbs in a thunderstorm about this attitude for years without any noticeable impact. They have been spending a fortune on glossy pamphlets depicting a big cissy standing on the back of the advertising agent's boat in some marina, looking for all the world suited and ready to go to the Foreign Office, and quite unlike anything or anybody that actually goes on the water. This gay venturer's enthusiasm for a day by the sea with Francis is clearly fading, and he usually has to be given a winch handle to hold to cheer him up, or gaze through a pair of 10 × 40 binoculars at the dockyard wall eight feet the other side of the camera. The manufacturers are equally inept with Ladies' gear as they are aware that very few good looking cookies actually need to get seasick making stew for six males, have buckets of salt water tipped over their hair, and be treated like latter-day galley slaves. Yacht clothiers therefore try to hedge their bets by advertising ladies' yachting wear with pictures of well rounded examples not wearing much of it, in the hope this will encourage the male end of the market to buy some for themselves and as an afterthought order a slightly smaller set for the old lady. Both approaches are totally wrong for a market which really wants discreet shabbiness.

Snotti Yotti Direct Clothing (Plain Wrappers) Ltd, on the other hand, is close to grasping a Queen's Award to Industry by buying ex MoD and jumble sales gear and processing them in a way which meets the market demand.

Their suggested basic clothing list is as follows:

	Male	*Female*
Cocktail dress: easily crumpled material – S.Y. Ltd treatment one diesel stain – salt impregnated zip – Sailmaker hand-made canvas evening bag to match. Optional extra: expensive diamond sea-horse brooch.	0	1
Ball dress: as above, but diamond brooch essential.	0	1
Reefer jacket: Petty Officer's No. 1s 1914–18. Buttons to order guaranteed soaked for three weeks in brine, patent green mildew overlay – one patch and two tears made good with sailmaker's twine – one button obviously fixed with split pin. Optional extra: cleaner's tab	1	0

	Male	*Female*
marked 'Instant Clean Antigua'.		
Trousers treated as above but carefully selected to not quite match.	1	0
One pair russet sailcloth trousers faded to light pink/white/grey patches.	1	0
One clean well cut pair of seaman's trousers with flap cut to fit hip and mid-girth measurement two sizes smaller than madam's.	0	1
Old flannel check shirts.	2	2
Selection of club ties carefully processed to indicate purchase prior to new supply being made in Hong Kong. Similar headscarves.	Neck 4	Head 1: (extra Snotti poking out of handbag)
Sailing sweaters, faded oiled wool, blue (never turtle neck) embroidered Admiral's Cup 1967/America's Cup 1964/Singlehanded Transatlantic Race 1972 to order. Stitching then unpicked to indicate modesty but enough threads sealed in to convey message.	1	Husband's spare
Sailing sweater, as above but embroidered with name of your yacht – recommended only where yacht values at £30,000 and upwards or is red-hot racing success.	1	8 (7 for crew)
Faded khaki sun hat.	1	0
Faded navy sun hat.	0	1
Towels, ex R.N. issue, keeping water from running down inside of impregnable oilskins for the use of.	6	6
Oilskins: S. Y. Ltd can supply linseed oil black oilskins for going to the club in light rain but advise a competitor's modern orange with Velcro and plastic zip ensemble if you pretend going offshore.	opt.	opt.
Swimming trunks – large baggy oversize knee-stretchers. (Use 2 sail ties if shape justifies.)	1	Dependent on figure
Yotting cap – advisable for large yotti owner (his boat, not him) or all owners drawing pensions. Never allow crew to wear yottin caps. (All S.Y. Ltd caps		

	Male	*Female*
specially marinated by guaranteed twenty-four hour seasoning treatment with our patent cement mixer operation).		
Seaboots – Plain black. Imprinted inside 'Stolen from (owner's name). [White, Green and Yellow oversize seaboots are not Snotti. They are widely used by Frenchmen and visiting Australians, but for Englishmen can indicate personality defects which if wrongly assessed by others wearing a matching pair, could prove embarrassing.]	1	1
All Purpose Sailing Jacket – Blue outside, red lining – boiled before delivery to make both sides similar faded mauve.	1	1

This is the basic list which applies to the majority of aspiring Snotti Yotties. Special requirements can be met, but I would advise care before deciding on any major deviations.

The exception to these rules is the owner and user of a large smart motor cruiser. If you are not sure if you belong in this category the acid test is 'do you have to employ a window cleaner?' If the answer is yes, you need a

Some of the major ocean racing deviations

completely different image and clothing to support it. The plate glass and 500 h.p. Snotti Yotti will never be loved and can only hope to create the right impression by ALWAYS looking as if he and his crew are on a cruise in *QE2*. An oil filter change should only be attempted at 0300 hours and even then making sure no-one is looking. Ladies aboard should never be seen to cook. Any maintenance on deck should only be attempted by the owner after donning a snow-white boiler suit, a cap with a Bombay Standard cap badge, and false beard and dark glasses. Yachting gear from Gieves, Balenciaga, Dior and Garrards.

For goodness sake be careful taking this type of yacht to sea. A brisk force 4 over the tide could damage your image for life, as the impression you must give is one of being able to glide across to Dinard for lunch and be back in Poole for dinner at the dear old R.M.Y.C. We can supply some accessories which will save you the embarrassment of pounding the tube out of the colour telly, risking Pheona's poodle being stuffed into quarantine for six months, or chancing the embarrassing discovery that all you have in the plastic radar dome is the remains of a case of Calvados.

Large motor yacht accessories:
(1) Basket with eight replica fresh croissants.
(2) One pair transfer 16 × 10 inch self-adhesive Union Jacks guaranteed to increase maximum cruising speed by eight knots.
(3) To fit eight-track stereo system: cassette recording Marine Band – 'Anchors Aweigh', 'Reveille' (muted), 'The Roast Beef of Olde England'.
(4) Accurate facsimile models that can be seen from twenty yards in the open steering space of the following:
    (a) Kelvin Hughes radar track plotter
    (b) Decca Navigator
    (c) Loran
    (d) Raydist
    (e) Omega
    (f) Inertia navigation system
    (g) Drawer fronts indicating world folio of charts
    (h) Courtesy ensigns for fifty-seven countries
    (i) Book with tooled leather *Norrie's Tables* cover: inside are simple instructions on how to get from Brighton Marina to Shoreham – Newhaven – Calais – Hamble to Cowes – Cowes to Poole.

Another exception is at the far end of the spectrum – the Old Gaffer floating history boys. Basically they should keep to the standard kit but may need:
(i) A Meerschaum pipe able to accept two and a half ounces of shag tobacco at one filling.
(ii) A knife in leather pouch made up from a Gurkha Churi-Ka-Pas and

some harness, and a marlinspike turned down from a fire bar. A piece of beeswax is also effective when produced with the loose change alongside an inch and a quarter galvanized shackle pin.

The one other exception to the general rig is the true round-the-world singlehander. He should never be seen in any gear other than a rather badly fitting plain grey suit with short sleeves or a massively oversize grey Norwegian oiled sweater, ragged jeans and bare feet. The former for yacht clubs, Squadron balls and visiting his family, the latter kept exclusively for round-the-world voyages and trips to London to see his publisher.

*   *   *

The sort of confusion which can be caused by not taking Uncle Adrian's advice was illustrated shortly afterwards by a sailing friend named Spud – Nigel's brother-in-law, actually – who was ordered ashore at Cowes by Mrs Spud to exercise the family terrier.

Muddly, as the terrier would not respond to, was a particularly good maritime animal and unlike most of his kind did not regard masts as tree stumps. Muddly would contain himself for so long as he was afloat and had been known to jump the last fifteen yards to land after a three day passage. Anyway, Muddly plus keeper were, as they say on 'Police 5', proceeding in a southerly direction on the east side of Cowes High Street and for some asinine reason Muddly's master was wearing a white boiler suit. This is the standard Yotti dress for the paid hand of large motor boats, and indeed one such was proceeding north on the west side of the High Street. He stopped to hoist in the combination of Muddly and modest example of Spud in Wonderland.

'Morning, mate.'

'Good morning.'

'I don't know 'oo you work for but the 'ands round here won't take kindly to you hexercising pets – we 'as enough trouble with our bleedin' owners without you lot from the Heast Coast coming an' givin' 'em more ideas. Use you loaf boy – poison it.'

Spud beat a hasty retreat down the passageway to the Island Sailing Club before an unofficial meeting of the Union of Motor Yacht Paid Hands South Coast Executive Committee could be convened and take action.

Dear David,

I have your letter and note that you would like to join a swish yacht club to match your new sailing image. You're quite wrong to think that it will greatly help for me to write for you, and as you have no need to join Brislingsea I attach some notes telling you how to do this yourself.

Yours sincerely

Possibly since the end of World War II, and certainly since the age of Harold Wilson's white-hot technological revolution, there has been a dramatic change in the social life of Yachtsmen which has not been generally recognized.

The widely held image of a Snotti Yotti is still one of a discreet gentleman of substantial means moving quietly between his secluded Victorian Club and his splendidly varnished ship – of calling for 'another bottle of club port' at one end of his journey and 'If you don't mind awfully, Ponsonby Smythe, I'm on the starboard' at the other.

Sweaty Knowles, your social statistician, made a head count from the balcony of the Island Sailing Club once, having found that he didn't have to put sixpence in the telescope, and without having to move his pint of Tankard he produced the following figures.

The average value of boat per trade of owner was: Retired Prime Ministers £100,000. Retired builders £87,000. Active builders £50,000. Scrap merchants £40,000. Inherited wealth £35,000. Company yachts

£30,000. Greengrocers £25,000. Wide range of trades in cash businesses £20,000. Doctors, dentists and solicitors £15,000. The vast majority of the rest £8,000 plus a thumping overdraft. Members of the Royal Yacht Squadron £9,845.

It would have been statistically nicer if Sweaty had included retired Prime Ministers in the classification of Squadron members to bring them up to a respectable average of ten grand or so, but he is suffering from a bit of a hump which has biased his scientific training. It seems it has taken him twenty-six years to train a maiden aunt to give him a copy of *Reed's Almanac* for Christmas, and nearly as long to get two bots. port from his godfather and a year's sub for *Yachting Monthly* from his mother-in-law. When all three plus his sister were seduced by the publicity for *Sailing* by Edward Heath and he got four copies that Christmas, he has since lacked a sense of humour about the book and its author.

You have, however, probably got the point. The ownership of grand yachts, and the facilities to discuss them in the grandeur of a Victorian

Club between the polished mahogany and the brass cupolas (with one or two historical exceptions), now involves two separate and distinct communities. One community is easy to join: you buy a thumping great yacht. The other is also simple providing you first swot up on the technique of how to do it without that horrendous expense.

Having mentioned the Royal Yacht Squadron, I may as well first cover that subject. Protected by a castle balustrade constructed by Henry the Seventh, the Squadron has remained unassailable. Treasure it as a distinctive feature of the Solent landscape: study the wrinkles of getting over the cruel tides on its starting line (always against you): accept any invitation to a committee meeting in the library or tea on its lawn: but DO NOT GIVE A THOUGHT TO BECOMING A MEMBER. If by birth, gentility or fame you are of a status to be invited you don't need my advice, and would be unwise to admit to any blood relationship with me.

No. In looking for a club try for one which will give you access to all the clubs you wish to *use* (not necessarily the one you join). Joining many clubs is expensive: therefore select one which will give you access to others, and the golden rule is that to use other clubs is more easily done when you trade down-market rather than trying to trade up. Sliding into the Royal Thames for dinner (however welcome the Catering Committee might find your custom) may be difficult if you tell the porter that you come as a visitor from the United Darlington Gravel Pit Sailing and Social. Far better to try 'Awfully nice of you to make members of the Royal Brunii & Northern Celebes so welcome'. As with obtaining a long line of credit from an Irish bank, both suits are better pressed if you have one.

The basic Snotti Club you need to join is therefore one likely to be easily socially acceptable to the ones you wish to use. Be careful here, and go some distance from areas of your normal operations. Flag Officers and Secretaries will be ecstatic on the South Coast welcoming you from the Royal Northern or Royal Yorkshire, but not necessarily as a member from the next club up the river.

Before thinking this is expensive, it is worth assessing the cost of a club against the benefits. You can take into account the certain knowledge that members who use their clubs eat and drink at prices subsidized by their fellow members who do not. The cost of breakfast, lunch and booze taken within the walls of the Snotti Yotti Club is certain to be much less than the same number of calories hoisted in on the open market at the Waterside Café or the Duck and Dog.

If you can afford to do the thing properly and join the right club, skip the next page which explains what to do if you can't, and jostle forward to the section of getting in over the heads of the present real, or fictitious, waiting list.

The Snotti Yotti image has persisted through an age which has changed the make-up of the sport. This has left some very odd anomalies of Victorian Elegance which are in fact cheaper than the membership of the local

T.U.C. Darts Club. There remain some very Snotti Clubs of which other Snotti Yotties have heard but few actually know what or where they are. The Royal Brunii & Northern Celebes would be a good example. Gieves can supply a magnificent tie and blazer buttons, the livery is good, the thing sounds right, and only a very few Celebians actually know that the clubhouse on its bamboo raft was washed a mile up a mangrove swamp in 1956.

When as a lieutenant I was doing my bit for Britain at the last Fleet Review, I sent in a launch to collect a retired Admiral from a jetty off Gilkicker to take him off for a few quick sharpeners before the fireworks.

Royal North Brunei & Celebes Yacht Club burgee and dress uniform

I noted the Yotti gear the Admiral had turned out for the occasion. The blazer had not been closer to the sea than Glastonbury Croquet Club for a generation, and the cap had been used to keep his tobacco out of reach of his cleaner for much the same time. The effect, however, was right and gave that slightly green, tarnished elegance cherished by the true Snotti Yotti. The Gothic letters on his cap badge had not been clear when embroidered in 1908, and ageing made them indecipherable: it seemed to me that here was a fascinating relic of some club on the China station which had been formed to help keep the drinking party going after the Wei Hei Wey races. Expressing this concept to the Admiral as a conversation piece en passage to Spithead, I found that Sir had not been Beattie's Flag Lieutenant for nothing, and was able to express (1) it was not the Wei Hei Wey Boating Club, (2) they were not Chinese characters, (3) the club was limited to officers who had served in the Royal Yacht *Victoria & Albert*, (4) this very select band of brothers took precedence over most, especially the years they elected God as Vice Commodore. This explanation was achieved in one sentence of eleven words.

The Royal Yacht Serving Officers' Club would be a very hard one to fault. If you have a Service bent, the Guards Household Division Y.C. is good too, providing one can pronounce Ws for Vs ('I'll have a wery large wodka and tomato'), and of course being able to wear a yachting cap on the end of your nose. As you are short of direct Service connections, don't despair: you had someone in the family in the last ten generations who went to sea or supplied salt beef to a dockyard, and stand a good chance with the Royal Naval Sailing Association. If stuck, you just have to do some research and I am sure you will come up with the 'Poona Polo Club Sailing Division', or the 'Khartoum Corinthians', or as a last fling adopt a mid-Atlantic accent and try the 'Prince Regent Sound Yachting Association'.

The only other form of antecedency which will serve your case is doing it the hard way, by joining a club or association of a select group who form a club to revel in their achievement. You are bound to get cold and wet in the process, but if you must: the 'Clipper Race Club', the 'Round the World Eastward Singlehanded Club', 'the Ocean Cruising Club', 'Rockall & Malin Windsurfers', 'Trans Mediterranean Pedallo Association' and, of course, the 'Joint Services Outward Bound Course of Surviving for More than a Month on Chay Blyth's Curry Club'. While not truly yacht clubs, the status of these 'specials' is such that it will daunt the Flag Officer of any club into thinking that they could hardly offend the natural successor to Sir Alec Rose, even if he does fracture the odd member's fingers when he shakes their hand.

While these are the general rules, there is one exception of an Exclusive Club which gives access to most others. It is well known that in the United Kingdom you are asked to leave a drinking establishment when the party is just starting *unless* you are a resident. There is, however, a back bar in a small pub on the South Coast which has two boxrooms upstairs. Anything up to a hundred and seventeen 'residents' have been known to share this accommodation for the privilege of continuing their sailing talk. Membership is purely based on the decision of the Landlord and your capacity to stay late enough to qualify. The only drawback is that club ties are purchased only from a store on Front Street in Hamilton, Bermuda, but it is well worth collecting one as the passport or secret sign of the Snotti Yotti fraternity.

You might think, quite wrongly as it happens, that your best course in joining a club is to ask your friend Trumpington-Jones who already belongs to do the necessary and propose you, fill in the forms, and get his friend Bill Ambrose to second you. This may look well enough, but the danger is that you can only tell the impression Trumpington-Jones creates inside the club by the one he gives you outside it. It could well be that he has anticipated this instruction and is well up in the art of the Snotti Yotti, and has succeeded in giving you the impression that only modesty prevents him from taking on the duty of Vice Commodore at such a youthful age.

The truth might well be that he became a member because of a secretarial mistake five years back, has had to be chased hard for last year's mess bill, and will never be forgiven for tearing the cloth on No. 2 Snooker Table the week before the inter-club billiards final.

The serious apprentice Snotti Yotti takes more care and on a visit to the club takes great interest in any of the varnished boards listing Flag Officers from 1946 onwards. (You might have to write to some of them, so make sure you have the right board and are not copying the Roll of Honour of the Great War.)

Follow this by signing in the Visitors' Book and making a check and noting the names of senior members who often sign in visitors. Swipe a race programme or other chit of club literature which has the whole hierarchy in the correct pecking order. Take an odd drink in the club bar, but be careful to give the impression that drinking with Trumpington-Jones is

Wing Cdr Trumpington-Jones

a little embarrassing to you, thereby hedging your bets in case he really did rip the cloth on the snooker table – or worse.

Having retired with these gems of information, wait for the next working day and telephone the Pru or similar ReAssuring Society and spin some line about 'needing to consider further life cover' or any story that will obtain their actuarial tables (preferably without an accompanying salesman). You can then set to work and divide your list of names into distinguished club members who on all actuarial authority must have turned up their toes five or more years ago – set this down in Col. 1. Members who are seemingly still influential runners – Col. 2. Undecided – Col. 3. In most of the better clubs you will find that a very high proportion fall into

Col. 3, and should you join, nothing afterwards will change this impression.

You then need to whittle down a short list, on the one hand of four or five distinguished, and hopefully deceased, Flag Officers whose names you must memorize. On the other, one or two Flag Officers who have signed in a good number of visitors, thereby confirming that they have an interest in the economy of the place and are probably either the Hon. Treas. or the Hon. Catering Sec. As a last shot for your locker telephone the club at 0901 on a Monday morning, give somebody else's name, and demand of the copy typist (who will be the only member of the staff there) in the best County voice you can muster, 'Tell me how many folk are there on our waiting list for new members?'

If she says 'None at all' reconsider the whole idea.

Now you have the ammunition, don't blast off without care. Select one of the Vice or Rear Commodores with a pin and set to work on him. Drop him a chatty little note on airmail paper and explain that 'When this assignment is over you might be in the area and have always wanted to see the club and might even keep a boat that way', that your 'dear old Pater was a great friend of Sir Jack Barker, who, if memory serves, might have been a member' and you're not sure 'if it was him or dear old Judge O'Sullivan who had suggested getting in touch with you', etc. etc. Give this letter to your Great Aunt Enid just before leaving to see the grandchildren her daughter produced with help from an incautious G.I., with strict instructions for her to post it while she is in New York.

Wait for three weeks and dash off another chatty note, this time regretting a delay in your schedule, and get some airline hostess to post it in Manilla. Follow up with one more mentioning getting in a bit of sailing, and have it posted in either Newport, Rhode Island or Sydney just before the start of the Bermuda Race or Sydney-Hobart whichever is appropriate.

At this stage you have created interest, and you can either follow up the approach after a month or so, or do it sooner, providing you are able to acquire a suitable tan with or without a sunray lamp.

You now approach the most critical test of the apprentice Snotti Yotti, where the knowledge you have acquired is analysed by long-term professional Snotties. You are therefore likely to be less vulnerable to exposure if you tend to say less rather than more, and to either feign deafness or buy a round of drinks if the conversation takes a slant of complete bewilderment to you.

Where possible keep the subject on general terms rather than attempting a technical discussion of I.O.R. Mk IIIA (it is unlikely, but you could actually be talking to one of the few people who really understands it). Suggested safe general talking points: (1) the sort of money the Americans/Australians/Japanese now spend on their boats thereby making competition in the sport quite UnBritish. Your audience will rise and agree at length to this. (2) You are not certain if some of these modern lightweight flyers are really seaworthy. Your audience will agree with you here as well, and if over fifty-five will tell you that anyone who sails anything not made of teak on oak strapped with three-quarter inch galvanized forged fittings is as good as admitting to be a maritime kamikaze. (3) Any reference to speedboats and/or waterskiing will immediately attract a discussion on people not observing standard Yotti conventions. (4) Your feeling that the planning request for the new marina is an excuse for permission to build a marine fun park/block of flats/licence to print money/or holiday camp, thereby spoiling the view from the clubhouse/select nature of town/old world charm of oyster sheds/fun of getting oneself bogged in a foot of ooze in the process of getting into dinghy/bring a lot of undesirables and distinctly non-Yotties into the place.

This is the stage where you have to throw yourselves to the wolves and get into the thick of the establishment of the Yotti Club you wish to join. Arrange with Trumpington-Jones to be drinking at the bar when the committee meeting involving the Flag Officers takes a recess from wrestling with the problems of reconciling the VAT returns on the bar takings with their visitor from H.M. Customs and Excise and they rush out for a refresher. If the Flag Officer you are courting held any Service rank above Army Captain call him 'Sir' at every other sentence and approach him as follows: 'Ahem. Major Knowles, didn't I drop you a note a week or so ago? The name's Creeper, Sir.' (Major Knowles happens to know why the VAT doesn't tally as he has been paying the cleaner and the greengrocer cash from the bar float since 1948 and any diversion which continues tô obscure this fact is welcome.)

'Good God, Creeper. Expecting you to turn up.' 'Very civil of you. A whisky if I may.' 'Cheers.' 'You know the Commodore?' 'Oh well, er, er, Jack Creeper, Brigadier Erstwhile Paycore.'

This is your moment: the varnished board in the lobby tells you that Erstwhile Paycore had two seconds and a first sailing Brislington-on-Sea One Designs in the undistinguished 1936 season. Seize on it with both hands. 'Well met Sir.' 'You know my father, he often spoke of a chap called Erstwhile Paycore who was an absolute wizard with those wonderful Brislington One Designs.' 'Must have been *your* father, I suppose. Had a fabulous run with them in the thirties.' 'Good heavens, not you.' 'Not seventy-four, Good gracious, you don't look a day over fifty.'

And so on and so forth. The immediate clique you are working on will realize that you are flattering the others, but think this amusing. They will not think the same of the flattery applied to them. As soon as possible get the subject round to joining the club without specifically asking.

'Hear you've just done the Sydney-Hobart, Creeper.'

'Well one fits in a bit of sailing when it can be slotted in. Actually hope to have a bit more time round these parts.'

'Hope to see more of you then . . . Oh, thank you . . . Same again please . . . Cheers . . . Now, old chap, why don't you join the club if you're going to be around?'

'I'm sure I'd like to be here, Sir, but really would like to get something fixed this season, and with a waiting list like yours . . . not really British to try and jump the queue. Besides, Trumpington-Jones tells me I wouldn't have a chance of joining.' (People will jump at the opportunity of squashing anything the T.J.s of this world expound.)

'Not really a queue, old boy . . . Really an excuse to keep out some of the newer sort we don't want too much . . . now while we've got you here you come with me and we'll sort this out with the Secretary.'

Without creating a scene, endeavour to have your cheque accepted there and then – preferably one which will be cleared. If this is in doubt, write next morning before your new friends have time to reach for the Alka Seltzer jar and confirm, with thanks, their efforts in making you a member.

Brother Creeper: you have just joined your Snotti Yotti Club.

*   *   *

Note This advice excludes the Royal Ocean Racing Club. That institution has had to accept for some time that it cannot limit membership entirely to Bona Fide Snotti Yotties. They have two problems at St James' Place. One is the practical one that to organize round-the-world 'bouncing from wave to wave' type races is so expensive that they require a huge membership to pay for the secretariat. The other is the fact of life of heavy ocean racing that the big boats need millionaire owners to pick up the monumental tab and a large team of hairy, fit and youthful gorillas to pull all the string at the same time. Even worse, both the millionaire and the gorillas have to devote all weekends and most of Monday and Friday to their sport. The millionaires are usually at a standard of business life when they can slip out of the office for a haircut without having to ask permission: the crew are not.

The heavies in ocean racing tend therefore to be unemployed or unemployable, or in the rare case when a heavy has gainful employment outside the boat trade he will be fired shortly after the Dinard Race when he is seen by his boss over there whooping it up instead of working at his cover story of fixing his flat after the fire/burying his Grandmother/nasty recurrent malaria/taking his sister to a clinic in Streatham, etc.

The RORC have therefore trimmed their requirements to suit, and only require an owner to confirm that the applicant has survived a couple of offshore races and doesn't get seasick (who the hell would want to join the RORC if they did), and get a Committee man to sign the chit. Offshore racing therefore creates a demand for a club which can accept a mixture of millionaires and enthusiasts living on Social Security. The RORC have therefore wisely stopped trying to be too Snotti Yotti and settled for this very practical formula embracing all real enthusiasts.

Owner taking his gorilla for a walk

Note Two The Royal Yachting Association is not a Snotti Yotti Club either. It is more like an admission that you are paying Yotti Income Tax, and tends to become more like the Automobile Association by trying to justify its increased costs by publishing newspapers or teaching you about baggywrinkles. It will no doubt soon follow the A.A. and sell its membership lists to people who try in turn to sell you anything from a safari holiday in Biafra to a free-trial-for-a-month male contraceptive pill. In short, it shows a good streak of Christianity to belong but won't do much for your image.

Note Three Make discreet enquiries before setting your heart on some University College sailing clubs, Medical School sailing clubs, heavy dinghy sailing institutions, or for that matter, the Strand-on-the-Green

S.C. or the Folly Yacht Squadron. The first three far from becoming a passport to better things will encourage the steward putting up the armour plate shutters quickly, and the latter two have a condition of membership that the participants have nothing whatever to do with boats.

*   *   *

Dear David,

I am pleased to learn my advice worked and you have joined the Royal Yarmouth Corinthians. As long as you look the part with a reefer and flannels there is no need to make a fuss about taking the rest of the crew in unless the club has been raided recently and they have got hot on the visitors' book.

If you're going into someone else's club don't slide in and look furtive – walk into the bar and ask for the Secretary or a Flag Officer – 'My name's Creeper Sir – on our way round to Harwich – Royal Brunii and Northern Celebes – mind if we have a clean up and a bit of lunch?' 'With pleasure, any time, etc. etc. Just mention my name and sign the book.' Good for four or five calls in a season, but don't push your luck.

The behavioural pattern of Yotties inside or outside their clubs follows the conventions of most Englishmen. Not to talk unless introduced, be gallant to old ladies, get to the bar and buy a round of drinks before anyone else but don't seem pushy, and drink at a rate which will not make you appear drunk faster than those around you.

There are no other conventions which apply to yot clubs, except that the conversation will be entirely Yotti. If you are learning the routine don't worry about the patter, just wait until the first hour of drinking is over and join in. The bar will then be so noisy that no one can really hear the speaker and will just laugh when he does. If you stand close to a good Yotti raconteur you will quickly acquire a fund of your 'own' stories. In fact there is no need to worry about telling the same story back to your donor. If he hears, a worried look will cross his face as he wonders if he lifted the story from you.

The dangerous Yotti talk is done in committees. Like other English institutions a Yotti Club is run by about ten committees. These work by Brig. Erstwhile Paycore and Major Knowles getting into a huddle over a pot of tea and deciding what is what. Major Knowles then briefs the Committee as to what they are going to decide. This sounds undemocratic, but suits everyone. Making decisions contrary to Paycore and Knowles will cause friction in the club; it saves any great thinking and the Committee meeting can then be turned into a good evening of airing views about the criminal idea of changing the rules to allow plastic Brislington One Designs (the speaker has just bought a very wet wooden one).

If you are invited to join a committee, or are proposed to be elected to one, give the matter serious thought. If you are a wizard at the Racing Rules they may genuinely want someone who understands them on the Race Committee. Watch it – as dangerous an occupation as judging the municipal baby show. Protests are held only between people of totally opposed ideas about totally irreconcileable facts which caused the incident. However nice the helmsman who loses is when he buys you a drink after you have found against him, he has you marked down.

Social Committee invitations imply that you have been earmarked to run the next Winter Fund-raising Dance. Catering Committee, that they would like you to run the bar when the steward is took queer in Regatta Week. House Committee, that your building firm might be quiet one week and slosh a coat of Sandtex on the front. And so on.

You will not offend over much by side-stepping all of these, until you get to the General Purposes Committee, which you can safely join as they will never decide anything but to refer items such as new crockery to the Catering Committee. In any case your place on any of these will readily be taken by one of the large band of either retired ashore Yotties, Lady Yotties who prefer the water in the club kitchen to that outside the breakwater, or 'buying a blazer and going down to the club looks better in the town than owning a beach hut' members.

In general, a splendid band who enjoy the mechanics of a yacht club, like being thanked for being Race Officer, love to hear the heavy Yotti gossip, know exactly who won the Town Cup in '62 and who went off with the Badgers wife in '66, and like to look a little disapproving when the wetter Yotties come back and a puddle leaks out of some foredeck pair of seaboots onto the club bar floor.

Treat them with the respect they deserve for making the club

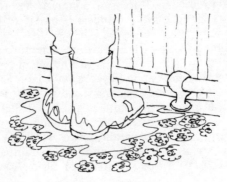

work and always thank the Race Officer for the trouble of organizing a good day's sport. Don't dream of joining them until H.M. Government award you a pension.

Yours, etc.

Dear David,

SAILING TYPES

In pursuing your new interest of social status sailing, it is wise for you to know some of the characteristics of sailing people, and whilst you can hazard a guess as to the social background of the owner of a 12 Metre, or for that matter, of a speedboat with five Union Jacks down the side, you should also know that the type of boat sailed by a yachtsman will induce additional characteristics in him in many ways similar to a dog owner who looks like, and acquires characteristics of, his pooch.

Old Gaffers This is a general description of a hardy group of yachtsmen trying to preserve as working models ships of an earlier age. There are two branches of Old Gaffers, the exotic ship preservers who become enthusiastic about keeping a Chinese junk, Arabian dhow or Dutch tchalk, or their mechanized brothers maintaining Admiralty steam pinnaces and launches, old working ships, tugs and so forth, and the conventional type who continues to sail a Thames barge, Falmouth Quay punt, Malden smack, Brixham trawler and so forth.

The cross they bear is a heavy one as maintenance of most boats is onerous, but when the timbers have seen the first hundred years it becomes a crusade. The amount of sailing they can do is hampered by the time they spend recaulking, fixing metal plates, cutting out the rot, tanning sails, placing buckets under deckhead leaks, and becoming students of entymology by chasing little wrigglers which vary from cockroaches to teredo worms.

For goodness sake never mention it to them, but their actual sailing is limited to the occasions when the wind gives them a free slant of at least eight points and is above Force 4 in strength, which is the minimum which will get them moving, to below Force 5 at which their spirit, jib-boom, upper topsail vang, leeboard or sails are at risk of showing their age.

The truth probably is that they really enjoy the maintenance and are somewhat frightened to risk destroying this hard work by taking the vessel offshore. Their working gear will include thigh boots, incredibly black overalls, tar brushes, caulking iron and an adze.

'Don't you think you're carrying this traditionalism a little too far, dear?'

This type of sailing is greatly enjoyed by wives as the exercise gets Hubby building a new oak leeboard, keeps him in fair trim, and the nearly static position in the mud berths allows Mrs Old Gaffer to tend to her pots of geraniums and to knit vast oily woolly sweaters which are intended for the often-discussed voyage to the Baltic, but somehow get used when they go down to 'do a bit of caulking' in December.

Major Knowles has the uncappable Old Gaffer story.

'Well you see, we wan this wegatta for these underpwivileged theacadets. Adwian took them to a clear piece of Tholent and left them to thail wound a bit. We had a couple of dwinks and a game of bwidge when a horwific line school came down the Tholent.

'Nigel dwopped the thails all on the deck, but this old gaffers' race that was going on all wound the Tholent disappeared in the wain and when it cleared the wiver was full of ships with top thails trailing off mathst, jib-booms pointing squiffy, stunsails, top thails and courses trailing awound evwywhere like commissioning pennants.'

Like all Major Knowles' stories, we thought he had finished but he hadn't. 'They got me on the Pwotest Committee.' (Not a very difficult exercise.) 'The wow wasn't the usual constwuction of the wacing wules but a simple port and starboard collision in very heavy wain. The man who was on port thaid he was wery thorry that his job-boom had gone thwew the other cutter, and speared it like a thword fish. But the damage had been caused not by the accident but because the other boat was wotten. The aggwieved man in the cutter on starboard said that all old gaffers were wotten, and the boat that hit him was a fwaud, and not only had it got itself covered in plastic but that the owner was using thynthetic baggy wrinkles.

'That's the nastiest thing one Old Gaffer can say to another and they both thtormed out of the pwotest meeting to instwuct their Tholithitors.'

FROM ADRIAN (CONTD.)

Multihulls Somehow ignoring the fact that people have been sailing around in multihulls in the Indian Ocean and the Pacific for longer than recorded history, the new owners of twin and triple hull craft like to give the impression they are in the forefront of yacht-ing technology. In fact they have much in common with the Old Gaffers, as easing a catamaran through the wind is very similar to the same manoeuvre in an old gaff cutter, where both types have to be sailed off the wind to get a bit of movement, headsails have to be let go, mains eased, headsails backed, the whole show comes to a grinding halt and goes backwards for a minute, the rudder is put a-back until the sails fill, and off both old and new can go on the new board.

The multihull scene, however, splits between the set who are from Southampton University Department of Marine Technology and are trying hard to prove that a boat can sail along without touching the water at all versus the larger group of multihull owners who have gone in for that type of boat as being the only way they can sell the sailing idea to the family on the grounds that it is really more of a luxury flat on the water and couldn't possibly tip over. The 'stable flat' brigade quickly find that tacking a small squash court or sailing it with one hull out of the water can be a terrifying experience, and they soon find a shallow-draft mooring and keep the boat there to the satisfaction of the wife, when it does become a floating flat and she can get some curtains on the large side windows.

The serious sailing set have found that to make their twins or triplets to go fast also means that overall weight has to be kept to a minimum, and they acquire a serious complex should anyone suggest the whole set-up could be dangerous and flip over. To prove how safe it is, they will have a large flotation chamber on top of the mast, two very-quick-release liferafts (one attached above the bridge deck and one below it), and automatic sheet-release cleats to let fly the sails when the craft leans over more than five degrees.

All sorts of multihull owners are concerned about the lightness of construction in their craft and will wince at heavy-footed travellers going across their decks. However much similar in style they have to be to an Old Gaffer, they will not be pleased if he threatens to tie up his smack yacht alongside one of their balsa wood floats.

'The problem with multihulls is the strength/weight ratio . . . '

Ocean Racing   Often thought of as the glamour market of sailing and relates to capitalism in the same way that ping-pong relates to socialism. If you want to be Editor of the *Daily Worker* or Chairman of the Newham Housing Committee, you're for ping-pong. If you fancy the Stock Exchange, Lloyds, banking or Conservative politics, you will be better proving yourself as a survivor in this aggressive and capitalist world.

When Brig. Paycore and I started ocean racing our fairly heavy boat was a conventional long-keel cruising boat. The new lads to the game would be surprised how it was not so long ago that all competitors deemed it wise to take their spinnakers down for the night.

To realize what has happened to ocean racing, you really have to understand the serious dinghy sailors, who have found that to make open dinghies go fast you need to keep the weight down and be able to change the shape of the sails as you go along. Having discovered these two basic ingredients, dinghies then go faster or slower dependent on the skill and ability of the helmsmen and crew. This has not stopped everyone else with a dinghy who is not winning feeling that the lack of success is due to his gear. Fashions therefore change depending on the successful boats of that season, and dinghy sailors will go from wildly complicated blocks with small pulleys to single whips round vast gin blocks at the drop of a few races in any open regatta.

Nigel was quite a good Hornet sailor before he got involved with *Lassitude* and had endless fun changing non-essential parts of his boat and then watching the rest of the fleet emulate them. His finest hour with Hornets was to buy up a job lot of instruments from a Javelin fighter scrapped by the RAF and build these into the side benches and then spend some very happy weekends quietly watching the rest of his Hornet fleet take surreptitious notes about his Aerofoil Attack Indicator, Drag Indicator, and Stall Speed Warning display. He sold the boat for about twice the cost of a new one.

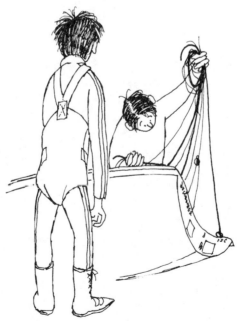

Dinghy men and their 'tweakers'

People who go ocean racing have themselves to blame, but due to importing features like Nigel together with his variable geometry sails and unbelievable number of extra strings to pull to achieve the right sail shape, they have changed the business in the last ten or fifteen years out of all recognition from the style of old Erstwhile Paycore and I sheeting the sails hard in and plunging off into a headwind with everything strapped down nice and tight. Not only have we acquired all this go-faster equipment but the changing fashions have caused us all to spend far more than is sensible. If Peterson has a few boats in Europe and there is no wind for any of the major races he is doing well, and if it is almost a dead calm Holland is doing better. If it blows a hooligan the traditional expertise of Sparkman & Stevens does rather better, and the wealthy owners change from one to the other to try to get it right.

The rest of the razamatazz of dinghy sailing has come with it, and increasingly participants try to bull up their 'team' image with matching sweaters, topsides, transoms and spinnakers highly decorated with their chosen emblems, and stripey boats which now

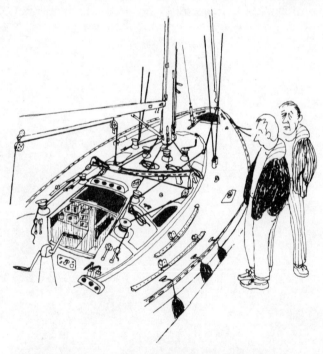

'Well, there was one chap who knew what it was all for, but unfortunately he left us to fly Concordes.'

look more like racing cars. Hot crews act increasingly like prima-donnas, expect excellent food, free travel and that their owners retain a truly British phlegm when they tell them that they managed to write off £1,000 worth of sails on the trip back. Masts are made to give their owners heart attacks when they see how they bend, keels are so fine and thin that they dare not go aground, and one of these very unfine days you may have a very nasty race and find some of the more modern boats will have the opportunity to see if the soggy black mess in their liferaft canisters does actually blow up when encouraged by pulling the cord.

To compound the problem of fashion, the rule makers are influenced by the world's sail makers, mast makers and designers, and just about every time a new rule is settling down there is a monumental change so everyone can have another five years of expensive enthusiasm trying to see whether short fat boats with big masts go faster than long thin ones with short masts.

There is no doubt that smoking is bad for you, but it is an addiction and so is ocean racing. Like smokers, one should not be sorry for people who spend a lot of cash on a self-inflicted disease. Ocean racing has produced a spin-off of much faster, cheaper and lighter cruising boats and provides a completely absorbing hobby for a number of very wealthy and determined businessmen. It is perhaps sad that by the time these men have acquired the wealth to be able to afford ocean racing in a big way they have put on a bit of weight and years, and it makes them a little distant from their youthful and irresponsible crew, but as their secretaries, telex machines, telephones and assistant vice presidents can get at them constantly for eighteen hours a day, seven days a week when they are on land, to escape and try to be as irresponsible as their younger crew is a great relief and stimulus for them at weekends.

Even in your new swish club you will not meet many of the owners of the top end of the ocean racing fleet. Their boats will be brought close to their helicopter pad just before the start of the race, and afterwards they will be escorted ashore by their eleven heavy crew who will encircle them and protect them like a rugby team allowing a change of shorts in the middle of the pitch at Twickenham.

The one exception when everybody meets everyone else is the Cowes Week of an Admiral's Cup year when you don't even have to name drop and will find the Dicks and the Olins, the Teds (Heath and Turner), the Nicholsons and the Mays, the Petersons and the Hollands, and Uncle John Illey and all nudging up for a quick beer at the back of the marina. If the brewers were ever to be as indiscreet and release the figures for the amount of beer sold there in that week, and you divided by the number of competitors (even allowing for the Australians and New Zealanders) you would discover that the consumption per head is too high to allow life to be sustained.

With the exception of the level rating boys, whose boat, crew and behaviour are exactly the same as a hard dinghy school, all other ocean racers are in one form or another family cruisers with a good set of sails who like having a go. The reason they like handicap racing is that until several days after most races it is impossible for anyone to tell how well they have done unless they win by a handsome margin. Everyone can therefore thrash around the Channel and feel they are doing quite well by going faster than other boats, even if the ones being passed have a rating two or three feet lower, and you will find that if you plough round some courses like this and don't make too many mistakes, there will be a bit of glory for everyone and your friend in the Conservative Club at Cirencester will not know that being third in Class 2 Beta Division in the Seine Bay race was no great shakes when there were only four boats in that division.

By a little consistent sailing you will find that apart from a few Service yachts or club yachts which are inevitably last, and a few whiz-kids at the top of the fleet who are invariably first, everyone else can quite honestly justify their largesse at the bar in saying that they are having a good season.

The Dinghy Fraternity   A cruising yachtsman goes down to his boat on Friday evening and is completely part of his ship until Sunday night or Monday morning. Any brush he has with the shore or his club is quite a temporary and passing arrangement. The dinghy sailor is the complete opposite, as there is a limit to the number of hours stomach muscles will allow him to hang leaning backwards out of his boat. Therefore most of the weekend is spent in or around the club with brief periods of pushing trolleys, wading, launching and racing. It is a sad result of this that the better looking girls are more likely to put up with the inconvenience of watching a couple of hours racing from a sheltered balcony, and thereafter be wined and dined in stable surroundings, than they are to go and cook for six men in cramped conditions in a boat which is heaving around on its moorings, or worse at sea.

By and large the dinghy fraternity do not approve of having this entourage of ladies nobbled by a sex-starved ocean racing crew or a group of bachelors who have gone off for a cruise on their own, and for this reason dinghy sailing clubs are normally created as separate entities from heavier cruising and sailing institutions.

The dayboat yachtsman that you find in the established yachting and sailing clubs, as opposed to the dinghy clubs, are a different breed. They sail boats which are either of an older one-design class or keelboats which they tend to keep on moorings rather than dragging up and down the beach, and have a club launch to take them 'awn' and 'awf'. The skipper of such a crew of three wears a yachting cap and is the only one to see any of the action as most of these older one-design classes involve the other two crew sitting below deck level in a puddle of bilgewater.

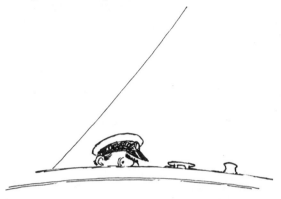

As well as the two hours sailing, the dinghy sailor spends a further two to three hours looking at the competition and changing the sail-tweaking arrangements on his boat. Not so the established one-design class racer who is in that business only because he and his fellows have strongly resisted any change. If Mr Prior or Mr Stone decided in the mid-'20s that the boom was sheeted that way, that's the way it's going to be sheeted in 1990. Forced changes such as swapping from cotton to Terylene sails, or building new hulls out of fibreglass, are tenaciously resisted. As the races are normally about two hours long, it gives the keel and one-design classes a great deal more time before and after sailing with nothing to do. They therefore tend to have florid complexions under their yachting hats, and have the time, and interest, to take on all sorts of functions connected with sailing clubs which provide an excuse for staying around the clubhouse during drinking hours.

Motorboat Owners With the exception of people who run racing powerboats, who are a specialist breed but somehow are never seen except for the week before and after the *Daily Express* Power Boat Race, and the owners of multinational companies who run a floating office/entertainment business in a slightly scaled-down edition of the *QE2*, all other owners and users of motorboats suffer from a slight complex, similar to that of Napoleonic types of small stature who have, or are made to feel that they have, to be a little aggressive to make up for the shortcomings in marine virility of their boats.

The truth is that most high-powered motorboats in their effort to look as much like a torpedo boat as possible are difficult to manoeuvre and park, and their full employment requires energy and experience. However, the marketing boys in the boat industry have very successfully created an image that all motorboats are incredibly easy to drive, and to make the newcomer feel at home have increasingly attempted to make the controls and way of driving such a boat as much like sitting in the front seat of a sporty car as possible.

As one of the great secrets of enjoying sailing is the feeling that you are conquering the elements, this approach has meant that motorboat owners have been conditioned into feeling that they do not have this satisfying challenge. But the ego has to be maintained, and the maximum ecstasy that can be obtained from a motorboat is letting the engines develop a huge amount of power to lift the whole boat off the water and create a great rolling wash. This fine feeling of power is best shared with others, so they prefer making the largest wash and splash going through racing fleets, up and down the Solent, and in and out of harbours.

It is really quite incredible that the vast majority of power cruisers are unsuited to serious seagoing work as they have too high a power/size ratio, very stiff stability, and very high topsides. And most owners have found that although their boat will go at twenty knots, it does not necessarily mean it will take three and a half hours to get to Cherbourg and that cruising offshore in the Channel is quite a difficult prospect. They quickly find it more fun to confine their energy to short sharp bursts in sheltered water.

Because the image of the big powerful sports cruiser is the one that leads the market, it is followed in style and custom on a smaller basis with boats for estuaries, lakes, rivers and canals. In a country where our Victorian grandparents knew how to build very practical, graceful and comfortable boats, for specific purposes, which for the sea were sea kindly, for the river had long, thin, sleek lines and low drag, it is amazing that we have lost that touch altogether and now have a uniform high-topside hull with a substantial

amount of glass plate deckhouse, and for everything over twenty-five feet a flying bridge. It just doesn't seem odd to the owners, or the market, that this is all a bit ridiculous when for most of their life speeds in inland water are limited to six knots and such planing hulls are almost unmanoeuvrable at that speed.

The motorboat yachtsman will, from this inability to satisfy his frustration, have a severe chip on his shoulder, and will suspect that you consider him a bus driver (even if you don't). He will nearly always confide that he would much rather sail but is prevented from doing so by sciatica, children, wife, available time or the necessity to be back by 9 a.m. on Monday. He will seldom admit to the fact that he and the family really don't like sailing or understand it, and are quite happy in their boat for the weekend and enjoy rumbling up and down the Solent because at that speed the bit that either they, or the wife, really dislike is overcome as quickly as possible, and they can more quickly settle down to the afternoon's fishing or sitting looking at other yachts in Poole harbour.

It is quite wrong, however, to take a disparaging attitude to such yachtsmen, but if you understand their weakness they will be delighted to help in some maritime roles, preferably of a salvage nature. If your engine breaks down and you need a tow, you are late for the start of the race and need to be taken out, you go aground on the Shingles, or need tools for a mechanical job on the engine, motorboat owners will be absolutely delighted to be asked for help.

Yours sincerely

Dear David,

It is impossible for me to give you any guidance about racing or the racing rules, and you will just have to develop your own technique after being beaten very badly a few times. With regard to the racing rules: in large boats these do not come into effect quite as much as in dinghy racing. They do need to be considered as the adrenalin runs that much faster when the prospects of collision are more dramatic. However, in *Lassitude* you are well served as Nigel cut his teeth racing Hornets in a competitive class where they either learned the rules quickly or were sunk: people honed in this field will flash protest flags at each other as soon as the five-minute gun has gone.

The less successful racer loves to copy the more successful, and the successful racing boys will get up to some mischievous tricks to stay that bit ahead. The story goes that one very noteworthy boat was attracting undue attention, and anything she did everyone copied. The three-man local crew became rather fed up with this and in assumed great secrecy slipped the boat and shrouded it from prying eyes with old sails. They then made a mixture of raw eggs and linoleum lacquer and put a sticky bottom finish on the boat, leaving her alone over lunch for the spies to sneak in and study the result, and the ingredients. The boat then went back into the water, was paddled quietly up the river to go alongside a wall, and they scrubbed the sticky mess off again. Starting the go-faster treatment but not finishing it slowed several imitators down for weeks.

But the uncappable story, of course, goes to the Grandad of Cowes racing, F. Ratsey, who in later life started to be beaten by some of the upstarts like young Uffa Fox. Whilst sometimes overtaken on boat speed he was never beaten with guile. He had the reputation of knowing the ground so well that he could short-tack up the coast to keep out of the tide in a rock-dodging way which invariably ended up grounding the followers. He particularly wanted to win one race in Cowes Week, and for several previous races the fleet noticed that Mrs Ratsey was to be seen bathing in her striped costume on the beach by the hardest piece of tide. Mr Ratsey was heard to say that he had arranged for her to be an early sort of depth finder as he knew he could always sail up to her when the water came to the bottom of the red stripe on her costume. He won his race: most of the competition went aground. Mrs Ratsey had been on the crucial station, with the water up to the red stripe on her costume, boats piled up all round her, swearing, pushing and puffing, trying to get off. Then she stood up.

You should have Nigel somewhere under the genoa leech telling you the rights and wrongs of oncoming situations and feeding you with gems about how not to get in other people's wind shadow and when to tack to create one for them. Whilst this is a gentlemanly sport, and Nigel will tell you where to go right when you go wrong, the person to have in the ensuing process is Sweaty Knowles. You may wonder why I have tolerated him in the boat for so long [We did, but this is not the reason] but he is an absolute wizard when it comes to dealing with protests.

What Lord Birkenhead was to the Law in making it simple and understood to the Man on the Clapham Omnibus, Major Knowles is in reverse with the I.Y.R.U. With a wide-ranging knowledge of the rules and previous decisions he will complicate any protest meeting on the most simple matter of a straightforward port and starboard into a case of such amazing complexity that all but the hardest and equally nasty protesters will apologize for having wasted the Protest Committee's time and retire immediately. As he has been telling other people that he is an expert on the rules for so long, quite a good proportion of people believe him, and like having a very senior counsel on a County Court trial, he will browbeat most committees into submission.

Whilst it is quite wrong to cheat, the rules are designed to be so complex that it creates an intellectual problem to gain as much advantage from them as possible. In the simplest possible form this is done by a game of bluff where two big yachts coming up towards each other have a right of way and give way situation, but that does not mean that the give way yacht need submit until he has put the fear of Christ up the other and made them stop concentrating for several minutes while they yell 'STARBOARD!'. Nor does it mean that when you are trying to get a clear wind from boats surrounding you you cannot create false noises and activity to indicate that you are going one way; having sold the dummy and got everyone moving to cover you, keep going as intended, or having played that ploy several times running, when you have convinced them you are bluffing you do what you say.

Nigel's cleverest ploy is on the fairly frequent situation of ghosting up a shore against a tide when you are limited in going too far into the shore by the depth of water and don't want to go out too far because of the strength of the tide. In such a situation boats going in towards the shore on the starboard tack have right of way, but on the way back out into the tide on the other board have to give way to those coming in. Nigel's trick here is with a kedge of minute proportions tied to a sounding line. On the way in on starboard you push out all the boats who are coming out on port; on the way out on port Nigel dangles his little anchor on or near the bottom and you shout that you are kedged to all the ones coming in. This will quickly create a situation where you work up to the front of the fleet and Nigel can put his little paperweight away.

Tight racing situations around buoys are inevitably complicated and no two or five boats will ever tell the same story at a protest. Before creating a protest situation you will find that Nigel and Sweaty Knowles between them will shout and quote rules about 'overlaps', 'distance from the buoy', 'sailing above your course', 'mast abeam' and 'water' with such powerful self-righteousness and conviction that any competitor in earshot could only imagine the Angel Gabriel wearing a sou'wester sagely nodding in agreement.

Lassitude is a big boat and no doubt the racing fleet now know that you are sailing her and have a limited amount of experience. If you take along a book of sailing rules and hold it up prominently in front of you as you tear up and down a start line asking inane questions of passing boats, you will find that the competition will tend to give you the benefit of the doubt and leave you a reasonable amount of open water to make your start – for this season at least.

Yours, etc.

Uncle Adrian pushed Edward Heath over the starting line during Burnham Week for reasons which were no more sinister or political than the fact that his yachting cap had temporarily fallen over his eyes while he was trying to steer and light his pipe at the same time. The distinguished owner had to sail rather farther that day, but still managed to collect the Town

Cup, and in speaking at dinner addressed himself to the Commodore, members of the Royal Corinthian and Royal Burnham, fellow competitors, and the owner and crew of *Lassitude*.

Uncle Adrian really tried to put him over the line the next morning, but got in a muddle in the process and went aground.

Dear David,

Rating

I note that under this new rule we have to get the boat re-rated and do not pretend to understand it. I do, however, understand measurers, and Sweaty Knowles understands the rating rule. If you get a blank form he will mark all the measurements that you need and indicate by a plus, minus or a zero whether you benefit by having a big measurement, a little measurement, or it doesn't matter. If you take your form round with the measurer and are extremely kind and polite to him, and Nigel is at his most helpful, between the three of you you will achieve the best result possible for a tired old boat, but I had better explain the whole sequence to you.

So that big boats can race against little ones, fat ones against thin ones, there has to be a handicapping system. The one we have been persuaded to adopt with other International Yotties rejoices in the name of the International Offshore Rule Mk IIIA. One hundred and sixteen measurements of boat, engine, spars and sails are taken and given by a rating office situated in Lymington to a computer terminal. This chatters away and returns a sheet of boggledygook with a myriad of numbers, the end product being a theoretical length. Boats perform in general as a function of the square root of their length so to finish up with a theoretical length is logical. It all sounds terribly clever and in the van of modern technology: so it is, but there has to be a human element, in this case the measurer.

Measuring is not a thankful task: if the measurer by some combination of errors produces a very good set of figures the owner will sneak off and not see him again; if the rating comes out high the owner will keep pestering the measurer until he gets a better result. This is particularly so in an age when level rating tends to attract people to build big boats and then try to get their ratings down to the magic figure.

Measuring is also a part time job which requires twenty-four boats to be measured or remeasured the second week in May, but not much work in October. The only possible source of labour for this task are retired Service officers. Very bright retired officers get themselves co-opted onto the local Electricity Council board or elected to Parliament or something. The middle range take on personnel jobs or run a launderette, and the remainder either try chicken farming or become RORC measurers, or both.

Measurers require a uniform which has to be a cross between rough sailing gear and a Boy Scout Master – the latter to emphasize the practical and pedantic nature of their job. The ensemble looks as though it should include green tabs sticking out of their long socks and a whistle on a lanyard.

RORC Measurer

The gear starts with a water-based level which is stuck on the back of the boat to measure the angle of dangle with a weight hung on the spinnaker pole. The Danglometer has pink liquid inside which has to be sucked out of the tube to clear the air bubbles. If when this is sucked out it is swallowed the mixture is Booths' Gin and Angostura Bitters. If it is spat out it is water with some cochineal raided from the measurer's missus' larder. The critical items to go with this are two plastic cans to fill with water to make the weight and some bathroom scales to weigh the water (the plastic bottles will leak slightly). The rest of the ensemble consists of rulers, tapes, and sets of plumb bobs and strings.

The 'instruments' are carefully unravelled from the measurer's car and in spite of careful preparation will become, like the honey-suckle, intertwined. The measuring will proceed with growing confusion as more and more pieces of gear get wrapped round their scientific partners or join in the mess on the boat. Measurements are taken to two places of decimals, often from datum points which have to be arbitrarily guessed to the nearest inch. Great deliberations are made as to who measures what where, round the delicate point of the lady known as the 'After Girth Station'.

With the boat ashore the measurer can only get his gear muddled up round itself: once afloat he has far more opportunity as he can let the boat drift round the measuring bay – with a bit of luck let it go altogether and then get in a super pickle in a dinghy hanging his weights on. The job is protracted when the wind tends to incline the boat more than his bottles, or he finds that tape, clipboard and pencil have all got where he is not.

Quite unlike Marina Masters, measurers have indeed much power over great boating investments and their owners: however, they use it humbly. They will be scrupulously fair, and will argue in a gentlemanly fashion when the owner tries to push a measurement his way. They will then write down what they thought of in the first place. The measurements themselves are suspect as it is not possible to work accurately with wooden rulers in a slightly choppy marine berth. The two places of decimals are too exacting for retired eyesight viewed from a dinghy.

I have always meant to write to the RORC about a proper inclining job. The training ship H.M.S. *Worcester* used to own the *Cutty Sark*. When it was sold to H.R.H. Duke of Edinburgh for a halfpenny there had to be some clever sums done to work out unusual stability calculations to lighten the ship as much as possible for her last voyage up a trench and into her permanent drydock berth at Greenwich. Two white chalk marks were put on her decks ten feet

'Well, look at it this way – at least you'll get maximum Inclining Factor.'

96

either side of the centreline. A pair of bathroom scales were placed on the gangway and two hundred boys were weighed and made to 'toe the line'. The angle of dangle was measured, the boys moved to the other line and the angle re-measured. Q.E.D. one set of metacentric calculations.

Providing the RORC could find large fat measurers for big boats and small wizened ones for small boats, instead of the Danglometer paraphernalia all inclining could be done by standing on the edge three, four or five feet from the centreline.

Yours, etc.

Dear David,

I suppose the rating you have got is as good as we can expect and all this stability measurement and age allowance has been brought in to make the older boats competitive, but I cannot really see it working and wish they could stop fiddling about and settle down with the rule.

In view of your estimate of the cost of a new mainsail and two headsails, I have been giving the basic rules some thought and think I have the concept of a real breakthrough.

The basic rule is now:

$$MR = \frac{\cdot 13L \times \sqrt{S}}{\sqrt{B \times D}} + \cdot 25L + \cdot 20S + DC + FC$$

If you look at the first function of this formula you will not have had to understand calculus at school to see that if you have a big length or a big sail area you will have a big rating; if you have a big beam or a big depth a smaller one. It is playing around with that combination which makes the money for Yotti designers, and if you look at the formula there is going to be a big advantage if you have no sails at all. A zero sail area will give you a product of zero for the first function of the formula.

If you think back to any Round the Island Race you will recall that the run down the south of the Island is made overtaking a number of beach balls which have floated out of their juvenile owners' hands off Ventnor Beach. As they go downwind they roll over and over creating very little drag, and for their waterline length go very fast.

If you extend this principle to a 40 ft diameter polythene heavy-gauge beach ball and have it rated by the RORC, both you and they will find that B. Max., Overall Length and Mid Freeboard will be 40 ft. Rated length will be about 22 ft. There will be a draft penalty, but it will get maximum inclining factor. The rating will end up at about 6 ft. The crew and you climb inside just before the ten minute gun, and with a bit of practice you will find that it can be steered across the wind by running up the side in the direction you want to make a bias across the wind: you can then maintain a course by keeping it going rather like the donkey wheel at Carisbrooke Castle. (There is nothing in the rules which stops you running about inside your boat.)

I admit that this craft will not be quick to windward, but dammit on a 200 mile race the good Class 1 boys will flash round in say thirty-five hours, but with your rating you and your crew will have an extra two and a half days to walk the course. I am not too certain how the racing rules apply when some clever Dick comes pounding up to you yelling 'starboard', but if in doubt you will just have to sprint for a minute or two and run round the front of him. The concept is also very safe: any nasty gale which may risk other conventional boats being driven onto a lee shore, with my concept only involves running downwind and straight up the beach to shelter behind a beach hut until it blows itself out.

Preference should be given to potentially downwind races like the Deauville Race, Bermuda Race or Sydney-Hobart where you can rely on a good reach or run, collect the trophy, deflate the yot and come home on the ferry.

Yours

'What the hell do you mean you think they're tacking?'

Dear David,

Thank you for the subscriptions you have arranged to have sent to me in this moribund isle. I will greatly enjoy taking in a whiff of the sailing scene from them.

Sadly, the editors of the various yachting magazines may not all be on speaking terms (in fact they are almost certainly not on speaking terms), but they do all abide by the conventions which are either imposed on them by the libel laws, or from fear of upsetting anyone who may advertise with them, or doing anything else which may spoil their quiet lifestyle. This is a pity as you never get from them the spice of sailing life – who went off with who's wife – how the Minister for Sport bitched up the Open Youth Championship – or why Sir Flogger Roundcourse's new £100,000 racer is as slow as an old pig.

What actually happens is that if you look at any of these glossies you will realize they could never print such a limited circulation work for anything like the cover price unless three-quarters of it is advertising. For the advertising department they need the best volume they can get in a specialist market, and with different slants try to offend no-one and be all things to all other men.

The format therefore gives you a glossy front cover, a wad of brokerage and other advertisements, then the main monthly theme whereby the editor expounds on the latest person, event or trend in the sailing scene which displeases him the most. The text then follows form to cover the big event, 'laying up', 'boat show', and 'fitting out' in the winter and, having survived the laid-up season, something about the big regattas and sailing in the summer.

It then goes on with something short to keep the 500 h.p. Mercury and sea sledge brigade happy, a General Interest article about a family/singlehanded/charter trip to the Seychelles/Brittany coast/eastern Turkey or the Grand Union Canal. The text tails off with small print articles about the goings on of the North Cape Sailing and Sexual Club, and in the same way as the local paper names the whole Committee of the Primrose League jumble sale, so do yachting magazines on the proven experience that putting a man's name in print is a great incentive for him, his mum and great aunt to all go out and buy a copy.

The theme then expires in a welter of small print advertisements which vary from 'Recently married owner forced to sell beloved 1901 gaff cutter, full Rentokil survey, must be satisfied that new owner will provide happy home for her' to the unromantic 'Yachtsman seeking blonde/brunette for extended cruise'.

Somehow the image these books create is one of a great enterprise run from the top floor of a huge glass tower block. When you analyse the content, however, there is little original copy not produced by the advertisers or purchased from a contributor for a modest fee. The truth will be that the editor and assistant editor share a desk and the services of a typist, who spreads her favours between them and the larger team who put out the *Gladioli Growers' Gazette* for the same publishing company.

One newly appointed editor did try to break the conventions, and actually allowed a very funny April Fool's joke to be printed which spelt out the dangers of a nasty beetle which ate fibreglass – a problem called polyestermites. So that these Yottimags have as long a counter life at the bookstall as possible, the April edition comes out in February, and a great number of fibreglass boat owners did not appreciate the significance of the cover date and wrote worried letters asking how they could dip their boat in some solution of polyestermites repellent.

Gladys from the *Gladioli Growers' Gazette* could not possibly cope with the influx, especially as they had done a special offer on gladioli mulch that month. The editor and assistant had to type so many explanations themselves that they have not since made any attempt to deviate from the norm.

Of course different magazines have different slants: a motorboat yottimag, a sailing yottimag, a cruising yottimag, and a dinghymag, and of course the very successful do-it-yourself yottimag. Personally I can never understand the appeal of a series of articles which tell you how to convert your B.M.C. 1100 motorcar into a paddle steamer; however, such a following does exist, and they love to turn Squeezy Liquid bottles into fenders, build their own true-motion radar sets, and at least know how to spend two years and a great deal of money making a ship's lifeboat look like a converted ship's lifeboat.

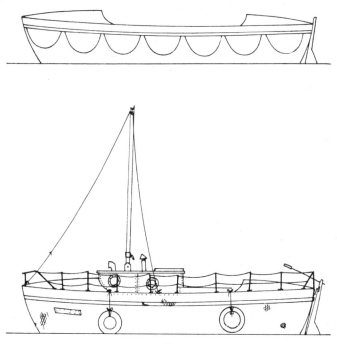

The one outlet that broke the rules was a weekly tabloid, which did give some gossip. I'm damned pleased it went bankrupt.

In addition to my monthly I will appreciate your letters to keep pace with what really happens.

Yours sincerely,

I showed the authority on yacht magazines to the assembled crew of *Lassitude* and would have had their undivided attention had they not been playing a serious game of liar dice to establish who was going to set me up with Rosie the cook that evening.

'Why did Uncle have a thing about that weekly yachting magazine?' I threw into the game.

'Nines on queens, the Great Train Robbery,' explained Nosey.

'You mean that the Arabian Oil Company was a front and Uncle Adrian was in on the Biggs business?' I slipped in, with the family loyalty for him inherited from my parents.

'Just shows how a story gets around,' offered Nigel in a vain hope that his hand of two nines and a load of rubbish might be mistaken for four jacks.

Having decided that Nigel had been elected into the honorary capacity of 'Chief Arranger of Nuptials for the Temporary Skipper', Nosey condescended to explain the story of Adrian and the Great Train Robbery.

'There was this bloke in Gibraltar who was meant to be mixed up with Biggs and paying the rent while the team were inside. It seems that he got picked up one evening by the Spanish Customs and decided that swimming was a better bet than a Spanish prison, but he was wrong as he sank. He had been living on a houseboat called *Lassitude*, and Reuters and *The Times* carried the story in a small paragraph, and it happened a week that that yachting paper had got a decided hole in the front page.

'Without checking the story they printed a full frontal of Adrian's *Lassitude* under the banner 'SAD END TO FAMOUS OCEAN RACER', gave details of some of the shadier sides to Adrian's past, and came close to suggesting that it was a bit sad that large boats could only continue on the yottin scene with the aid of the Mafia.

'The conversation Adrian had with the proprietor and editor has been quoted in the trade as the classic example of being able to swear for ten minutes without repetition, and of course they and their lawyers covered themselves with a long-winded apology which anyone with good eyesight and a magnifying glass could read in the next edition at the bottom of the "Retired Cattlefood Salesman and Wife require job lazing about the Mediterranean in Luxury Yacht" column.

'In the way of such stories it did of course stick, and a few weeks later we had one of those really disastrous days racing on the Solent and the big boy caught round the tall boy. The spinnaker fell in the water, we bent a spinnaker boom, and retired hurt to Cowes with the foredeck being very nasty to the cockpit, and the owner being nasty to both. We would have retired for an evening's heavy drinking to repair the alliance, but Adrian had already paid for tickets for an after race dinner at a very Up-Yotti Yacht Club, and in view of the bent boom, the torn spinnaker and general bloody-mindedness he was preaching economy among other things.

'We sidled into the club too late to have any sharpeners before dinner, and had to miss the soup and jostle onto the end of a sprig for dinner. Light subdued chatter went on about "If the Skipper had held her down-wind a bit longer I think we would have got it sorted," . . . "Ha! Flaming ha! Halfway up Lee-on-Solent promenade, and you would still be swearing at each other at Alton" . . . and so forth. This would have gone on all night had not your Uncle picked up out of the corner of one ear his lady neighbour telling her neighbour in nearly a *sotto* whisper:

"That one with the beard and the other one . . . were the ones . . ." flick of head towards Adrian . . . "mumble . . . mumble . . . George Biggs . . . Great Train Robbers . . . smuggling in Algeciras . . . fancy in this Club."

'Adrian was drinking whisky and water disguised as to quantity by taking it from a pint tankard; he went very red, and took a powerful draught of half a pint or so. His look of sailing depression faded into that sort of jovial malevolence his friends and crew know to be the start of a whole load of trouble, and when wise retire from the scene quietly.

'"Do you think," he said in a firm voice to Nigel, "Jimmy the Weasel will get full remission?"

'The first four places up the table fell silent to take in the next bit.

'"I would think," said Nigel, picking up the very pointed cue, "if he goes on with this monopoly on snout at Albany, he will be able to buy his way out."

'The whole sprig plus one on each side shushed to clutch on to the conversation.

'"Ha, very good," chuckled Adrian to an almost hushed room. "Did we say we would sail over to see George this weekend?"

'"I suppose we ought to go, but he's going to be very nasty when he finds out how much he's lost on consols." Nigel displayed the thought process with a smile and added, "George will say that's daylight robbery by the Government."

'In the loudest possible theatrical whisper Adrian put the knife in with, "I think we should go back to talking about sailing. The lady in the green dress could be listening."

'The cares of the day's racing having been buried, the evening was completely made for Adrian when he watched the lady in the green dress rather obviously take off her earrings and necklace, fold them in a serviette and pass them up to her husband for safe keeping.

'Nigel was told to brush his hair, and complete the evening by dancing closer and closer with the good lady's daughter, while the horrified parents contemplated the prospect of relatives by marriage in Pentonville Prison. Father was eventually placed under orders to break up this potentially disastrous liaison, but being British he avoided a confrontation and sidled up to Nigel and explained that how awfully sorry he was but had to make Cynthia a runner now as she was "racing" tomorrow.'

We never did kill the story, and for months were approached by people in bars who wanted to get some money out to Spain, or buy Swiss francs, and were all rather fed up with the Bonny and Clyde image when Nigel discovered that the story was so well entrenched that he was offered unexpected credit by his bank and from a series of winks and twitches gained the impression that the manager was quite satisfied with collateral of an assumed suitcase full of the stuff tucked away somewhere.

At this stage of a rambling correspondence there had been some mutiny from the crew, who had written a Christmas card to Adrian and suggested that if his health was not making a lot of progress they would have no objection if he wished to improve the potential performance of his pension fund by selling *Lassitude*. This provoked a very pained reply from Adrian, who seemed to think the idea desertion of the worst kind, and to salve the hurt Brig. Erstwhile Paycore flew out to Malta to have a short holiday with Mrs E. P. and talk about it. While they came to an agreement as to what to do, they both drank so much that Brig. E.P. came home without knowing quite what the agreed plan was, but it sort of involved buying a new boat which was smaller and more attuned to the I.O.R. Mk III Rule, the plan being subject to first selling *Lassitude Mk I* before paying over the cheque to build *Lassitude Mk II*.

Further confusion was created at a crew party around Boat Show time (once upon a time you could actually go to the Boat Show and buy a boat to sail that season), and from the nine serious sailors who came to the party there were ten propositions as to what type and style of boat should become *Lassitude Mk II*. (Nigel proposed a Nicholson 30 before dinner and a Hustler 31 after dinner with equal conviction.)

Yachting magazines were soon carrying advertisements which were a variation on the theme:

Ocean Racing Yacht of Great Character, Great Racing Record [she had entered a lot of events all over the world], 54 ft ketch, very full sail wardrobe [some were not shot], full electronics [one of the first experimental sets], 12 berths [to include the two sail bins], fine interior panelling [behind Nigel's *Playboy* centrefolds], Perkins diesel [tucked down over the keel], and the indisputable feature of the craft: Owner's private cabin aft with DOUBLE BERTH. Quick sale required at sacrificial price of £32,000.

Some heavy advertising produced offers, one of which the broker thought he could wangle up to £16,000. A lengthy correspondence between me, the broker and Adrian, and in April we had another crew meeting where it was decided what a silly idea it was to think of changing as we probably would not be able to sail one of these modern flyers anyway.

Adrian was delighted, and ordered a new suit of sails. His notes on Yacht Brokers follow.

Dear David,

Yachtbrokers are necessary to sustain the industry. They sometimes have an image akin to their land-based cousins, estate agents, and tend to form associations, mutual aid pacts, and image-promotion schemes to justify charging about three times more.

They do perform one extra function in that as well as finding the buyer they also arrange to convey the title, so you do not have to pay a marine solicitor as well. (Marine solicitors are involved in insurance and eat up about 30% of premiums in limiting claims on loss to about 50% of what you think you are insured for.)

Yotbrokers do have their own language which in print is Yottibrokeradvertese and the rough gazetteer below will give you the general idea for translation.

Yottibrokeradvertese	Meaning
A. Actively on the market. Admiralty construction converted to present high standard in 1950.	We are acting for the Official Receiver. It does not say which war the craft had been built for.
B. Boat of Great Character	Loose caulking, rotten planks, soft deadwood, fittings pop off the deck rather easily.
C. Comfortable 8 berth accommodation in 4 separate cabins	The boat is divided up like a honeycomb.
D. Double suite in Owner's Stateroom aft	A 5 ft 6 in × 2 ft 8 in berth is suspended between the gearbox and the cockpit floor.
E. Extensive electronics	Ideal for a BSc Mech. Elec. to try to get all working again.
F. Fast sports cruiser	Which uses £148 worth of fuel to go to Cherbourg and back.
G. Great racing potential	Four good owners having tried hard but done no better than a lucky fourth in the Irish Sea, but stripped out like this it will be hard to sell as a 'cruiser'.
H. Handles easily	Except on a shy reach when you need six strong men on the helm.
I. Ideal cruising boat	It's big, heavy and really slow.
J. Jumpher diesel 500 long stroke, hotpoint start, plus Lister wing engine	The wing engine was fitted for a very good reason.
K. Kelsholme Robert-Bluenell-Buchrose design, 1948	And he learned quite a lot from this one.

L.	Luxuriously appointed	The plywood bulkheads are teak trimmed and there is some soggy carpet on the cabin sole.
M.	Magnificent Club yacht	Has been sailed hard by club members for 27 weeks a year for the last 11 years.
N.	Now for sale as owner building larger	The poor chap has got the new one finished before he realized how hard this would be to sell.
O.	One careful owner	He has been very careful in spending any money on this boat.
P.	Perfect for ocean cruising	It needs a big sweep of ocean to tack.
Q.	Quality yacht, built by us and carefully maintained in this yard	Not only did we make a profit building her, but she has produced £1000 p.a. ever since and we now get brokerage as well. Super.
R.	Reasonable offers	Preferably what the owner considers reasonable, not you.
S.	Stainless steel rigging	Actually that is all we could think of saying about the equipment.
T.	*Tchalk* of great character	The bad news is that she has rot. The good news is that there is one hell of a lot of heavy timber yet to go.
U.	Unbeatable price, Boat of the Show in 1972	In 1972 it had a fine finish. Needs a repaint now and we have never tried to get so much for one of these before.
V.	Very suitable for enthusiastic youngsters	You would need to be young to put up with the deck leaks and enormous amount of do-it-yourself work this one needs.
W.	West Indies cruising and charter yacht for many years	And has brought back some very interesting tropical wrigglers.
X.	Xanthoxylum planks on Gaboon frames	We want to start off here with a moral advantage over the surveyor.
Y.	Yacht sadly offered at a sacrificial price	When she sinks on her mooring this will become even more sacrificial.
Z.	*Zubernubbi*, one of the first of the successful Star Class	And when they had built another six they had sorted out some of the problems.

The reading of Uncle Adrian's treatise on Broking was interrupted by Major Knowles with his story of Nigel, the one-time super Broker. 'Did

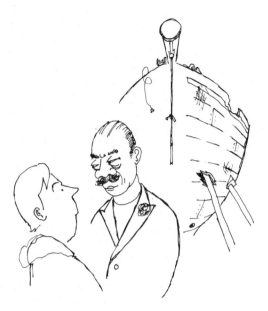

'Teak below the waterline . . . really well built . . . a yacht of great character and in remarkable condition for her age. Just between you and me, old boy, I'd say he'll come down quite a lot.'

you know that dwedful Nigul put up an awful black with his couthin Angela Dalrymple-Rivers?'

Nigel's social disgrace had it seemed stemmed from a brief but glorious period as a yacht broker. By some dint of standing at the right place at the right time, a very scruffy Greek had sidled up to Nigel at the Boat Show, who followed him onto the boat for no better reason than that the last prospective customer wearing a shabby yellow raincoat had behaved very badly in the shore-based marine toilet.

Nigel did his best to get rid of the man as quickly as possible by dwelling on the boat's unbelievable price tag. The Greek shipowner finished a brief tour and wrote a draft for the full price, and offered Nigel the delivery job for an additional sum which sounded like two years' gross income from his tea bar.

The Broker Boss was absolutely delighted with the £23,800 commission, and produced a large wad of notes for Nigel with instructions to take his client out for dinner and (wink wink) 'Lay on a good time. Couple of brunettes – you know the form, what.' Nigel hoisted in the idea even if he did not know the form, and having counted the wad in a nook behind the Guinness stand went off to telephone a friend on the Stock Exchange to get the number of the right sort of escort agency.

107

Having suffered some chaff from his friend at the Stock Exchange, Nigel booked the table at the Dorchester, and arranged to meet the girls whom the lady at the Earls Court Agency promised would be quite up to the occasion. After a couple more celebration pints of Guinness, Nigel was overcome with pangs of conscience. He was after all Church of England. Mrs Nigel was after all heavy with child. It would leave a much better net profit if he roped in Angela in lieu of Escort No. 2. He was just about sober enough to do a deal with Angela and cancel the additional escort.

The evening was a magnificent one, sadly missed by Nigel who passed out between the soup and fish. The shipowner, of course, went off with Angela Dalrymple Rivers, and the other kind-hearted girl took Nigel home to sleep it off.

The next that was heard of Angela was a postcard from the Riviera two months later, and Nigel's Aunty was very huffy about the whole thing. Gradually, however, the family came to appreciate the fringe benefits of her new lifestyle, and it was even suggested that Nigel might like another go at a Boat Show to see what he could do for Angela's younger sister.

'I think Nigel did rather well, Sweaty.'

'But thas not the point Dawid, thw wotten chap didn't ask me to go with him when he took the boat down to the Mediterranean, he went awf with a dwedful bunth of youngsters from a uniwersity.'

YACHTBROKERS (CONT.)

All brokers like to give the impression that they are really only involved in dealing with yachts in the mini-*QE2* bracket, and any lesser craft or commission is a favour they only undertake for friends. To confirm this impression to their friends, their rivals, and themselves, they vie with each other to take the biggest and best spaces in the yachting magazines to show off their prosperity by having the biggest and best advertisement.

They are quite decent to each other by swapping details of boats they get on their books, but once the first flood of passion at earning the big commission has passed they are not so good at up-dating the information. This is why in any one magazine you will see the same boat advertised in great (and largely different) detail by a number of rival brokers. The coy will not mention price: on the opposite page it says 'Try anything like an offer'.

The agent you need when you are buying a boat is the one who is handling the sale of the one you want to buy. A more subtle statement than it sounds, as if the one you approach is not handling that boat he will make a plucky effort to sell you one he is handling. The agent you need when you sell is the one who finds a buyer for you.

In defence of brokers, they do suffer from a general public who assumes that they run a free service and would not dream of paying for expensive literature which is demanded by the ream with no real intent of using it for the printed purpose, and a general public sentiment of being willing to pay the commission when the boat has to be sold which dissolves rapidly when the boat has been sold.

'Good God old chap, you are not suggesting that I owe *you* £800 commission for selling my boat to my old school chum Trumpington-Jones: we were at preppers together.'

'No, no, you did not introduce him to me . . . I introduced him to you.'

The courts are not very kind to brokers with commission cases, and brokers suffer the disadvantage that somehow boating folk know most other boating folk.

The other snag is that whilst most buyers know what they want to buy, few tell the agent what they can afford to buy. Buyers therefore join the same game of giving the impression that they are in the Amey to Aristotle bracket, when in fact they could just afford a pre-war Hillyard. All brokers will tell you stories of the chap who said he must have a Class 3 ocean racer and bought a fifty-foot concrete ketch. This explains why whatever sort of boat you suggest to a broker as being your forté, he will send you details of fifty-foot concrete ketches.

The one other function of yachtbrokers is to overcome the problem of democratic societies who do not allow sufficient wealth to be accumulated to buy the boats they manufacture. This has become especially critical to British brokers selling our yachting assets abroad to bolster the sagging pound. The game is not really one of deceit, but of creating such obscurity as to the ownership of a yacht that any tax inspector in Italy will run out of his allotted three score and ten before tracing the title back to the fat chap who sits on the back of the boat in Santa Margarita.

Therefore a West German businessman will, through his company, place some money on deposit in the Cayman Islands Maritime Bank; the bank will make a loan to a company with a registered office over a tea shop in Lichtenstein, who register the title of a ship in Monrovia but in turn take a leasing agreement on the purchase price from a registered shipping company in Gibraltar, who in turn pay the crew and charter the craft to a West German businessman for three Deutschmarks a month. Commission to a broker on a £300,000 boat may seem huge, but if you can sort that little lot out, after first unscrambling the seller and then rescrambling the buyer, it becomes very good value to all parties.

A large chunk of cash in the form of a registered ship is also a fine way to move capital around, and as you clear out of the United Kingdom the Customs man looks at you severely and asks if you have more than FIFTEEN POUNDS IN ONCERS as any excess is an offence. You haven't and say so, give him a wave, and move a football pool win turned into a British registered ship off from the quay and away from the jurisdiction of your friendly tax inspector.

Yours, etc.

Dear David,

YACHTCHANDLERS

You need not apologize for the bills. Boats are avid consumers of money and you do not seem to be buying other than practical necessities.

It is surprising that few sections of the boat trade succeed in hanging on to much of the money they handle, but you would think that chandlers must coin the boodle. You go in for the smallest trifle, part with £15 and come out with a couple of fathoms of cord, two shackles and a small tin of paint. (Whilst a chandler has to have quite a good mark-up, he does also have to have a whopping stock, and a big chandler with £100,000 on his shelves needs 3,000 sales like yours to cover the interest on his stock.)

'A shackle, my dear sir? – good heavens, no.'

The great saving that can be made with chandlery is not, as you suggest, to try to buy the stuff wholesale, but far more effectively by not buying so much. This is achieved by not losing too many winch handles, silting up marinas with shackle pins, or baking plastic plates and cups. However, the biggest saving of all is to part with as little as possible when you sell a boat, and discourage your broker from listing a 'fabulous inventory'. If you work this out, stripping your old boat will be a great saving on the new one and has the advantage of not harming the trade: the purchaser of your boat will just have to support it instead of you.

Any sympathy to the yacht chandler should be limited to those who do try to stock what you want. There is another element who are in the 'cash in on the yachty' class, and whilst they are difficult to define, and come in various forms, they will tend to go for quick-turnover stock. They will sell lamps but not wicks, new rubber dinghies but not patches for your old one, a row of huge outboard engines but not a pin for the shaft of the one you have just broken, a wall of small fittings, but no stainless nuts and bolts

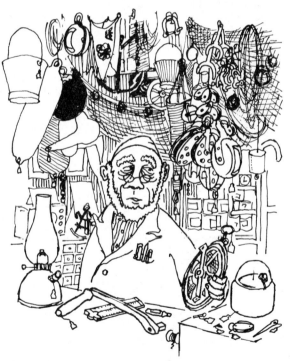

The ideal chandler: 'Last one in stock, Sir – not much call for astrolabes these days.'

to tie them on with. They will sell yachting caps, seashells turned into ashtrays, and have two new and one secondhand speedboat outside at prices you would have thought would buy all three.

It saves a lot of time and stress to avoid them altogether. If you do foolishly think they will help, you will find that of the five things that you want one is out of stock and they tell you there is no demand for the other four. If it makes you feel any better, ask them if there is a chandler in the town.

Yours sincerely

Dear David,

Y<small>ARD</small> B<small>ILLS</small>

I would agree with you that we seem to have acquired the most valuable forehatch for *Lassitude* in the history of offshore sailing. I do not think it will do any good to drip too much about this bill, but it will be wise for you to understand the boatyard system for future reference.

This bill has been inflicted by a big boatyard: the only other kind is a small boatyard. Big boatyards can be identified as having an office and a car park with a number of reserved spaces for directors. These cars will all have to be offset against taxable income so there will also be a substantial accounts department, who run a slightly independent business to the one the yard manager and assistant managers think they run.

The yard will also have one or more unions, shop stewards and negotiating procedures, and they work in a business which they consider to be different from both the accounts and the management departments. Finally there is a retired rigger who has kept the 'old man's' job in the yard as the gatekeeper and who made a swing for the managing director when he was two. He is the person to know, as whatever other sectors of the business think they do, Nobby at the gate actually knows what they do, and more important, will greatly enjoy telling you how to go about getting them to do it.

If, as in the instant case, you telephone the assistant yard manager and tell him that a big wave broke your forehatch and would he please repair it and make it stronger, he notes this down on a telephone pad and tries to avoid your further request of *when* it might be done.

Although his intention was to get down and have a look at it during the morning, all sorts of crises accumulate and it is 4.30 before he gets to have a quick look and assess that it is a shipwright's job. He potters back and does a work sheet, top copy shipwright, second copy accounts, third copy storekeeper, fourth and illegible copy on a mounting pile on his clipboard.

The shipwrights are busy next day and it is not till the following day that the foreman shipwright has a look. He does some measurements and decides that it is going to be tricky and will need a new hatch top, that they are pressed and will have to get a drawing and sub out the work of making the new hatch. He memos the manager that it needs a drawing and could they sub out the cover and frame.

A spotty lad from the drawing office is sent down to make a sketch and take some measurements and spends the rest of the day making a beautiful detailed drawing which he signs in pseudo copperplate and makes several copies of for posterity. This is posted to a firm of coffin makers in Little Melksham who make some outside joinery for the yard when the coffin trade is slack.

The owner in the meantime is beginning to fret, is given re-assurance by the manager's secretary when he telephones, and all managers from this time on will be hard to contact by telephone.

A week later the component parts of the new hatch come back from the Cheerful Timber Company Ltd, and the shipwright walks down to offer them up and size up the job. He is a craftsman and realizes immediately that either the spotty designer has muddled up his measurements or the joiners have read the plan upside down, as there is no way that hatch will fit the beds of the old runners.

He therefore goes to see the manager to complain of the additional cross his team have to bear as a result of the rest of the firm's incompetence. The foreman would prefer the whole job to go away for a week or so more, but the manager realizes that he will not be able to avoid the owner for that time, and they go down and the foreman is flattered into using his real skill and works out how they could make some new hatch runners to accept the new lid.

This would be put in hand first thing next morning, but when the chippy and his mate arrive they find that they have to move a run of wiring to unbolt the old hatch, and the inner forestay has to come off to give them room. This involves the electricians and riggers (who are both busy), but further work sheets are issued and the job is cleared by the end of the day.

In about two and a half hours next morning the chippy and his mate cut, offer up, fit, finish and make working a beautiful pair of hatch runners and the whole thing slides like a dream. The one thing they have not got is a catch that will lock the new design. They explain their needs to the storekeeper after they have lined up at his service hatch. He looks in a catalogue and decides they want an SN L564 a, which he notes and orders.

As the paperwork is going on to get the SN L564 a, further work sheets are issued to get the wiring back in place and the inner forestay set up, and the painters get a slip to put on two coats of varnish.

As the job has now taken nearly three weeks the owner is getting apoplectic, but the managers are talking to him again as they can safely say that they have now been held up by British Industry and are waiting for a forehatch clip. At lunch the owner wanders into Captain Watts' shop and sees a great heap of them on the floor, buys one, and sends his sales director off early for a long weekend and so he can deliver the clip to the yard. The one the yard ordered arrives half an hour before the expensive one, and is fitted that evening after the manager has sanctioned a couple of hours overtime.

It will take months and months for the accounts departments to break down from all the time sheets from six departments and the stores how much this is to be charged out at. The final cost will very much depend on what the individual tradesman wrote on his timesheet. Seldom do they deal in fractions of an hour. If the rigger boarded the boat and took off the inner forestay while explaining to his mate how to get carrier pigeons to mate, he will not book anything up and this service will be paid for by some person whose mast is being stepped. If he remembered doing your job at the end of the day, but was talking about pigeons when rigging the other mast, you may get four hours.

Far worse if the boat has a reputation for sailing, or the outrageous behaviour of the owner has ever received any publicity, or it is a new design or of a new material: it will attract goofers from the whole yard. Having expressed interest in the boat by paying a courtesy call they will justify this interest by sticking her down for an hour to justify their courtesy visit.

In the bleakest part of January you will eventually get the bill which has been simplified for you by the accounts department.

To rebuilding forehatch, June.

Materials	54.62
Design work	44.00
Labour	629.75
	728.37
VAT	91.05
	£819.42

Account with Compliments

There are three ways round this situation, which will not make the job cheap but will limit your liability. The first is to think of some excuse which only allows the boat into the yard for a very short period. Getting it all done in twenty-four hours will be quite feasible and limits the number of hours that can possibly be booked onto that job.

The second is to go and see the manager, and with him the shipwright foreman, and discuss with them how the job could be done, bearing in mind your poverty and inability to pay anything more than £85. If you strike the right chords you will eventually get it done for £120.

Finally, the best method is to use a combination of both the above, plus being in the yard yourself. With the aid of the gatekeeper you will be able to slide into the various workshops and ask for Tom, Percy or Bill the foreman, and get them on the job in the correct order and time. Giving each crew a beer as they finish the job will limit the pain they are willing to inflict on your time sheet at the end of the day, and whilst everyone will be nice, they will find that your frequent visits make it easier to do the job than have you lurking about.

In January you will get a bill for about £80 and the accounts department will have a full-scale internal inquiry to try and find what went wrong.

Yours sincerely

Dear David,

SMALL BOAT YARDS

In my last letter I explained the organized approach you need for a large boatyard. You need a quite different tack for the 'man and a boy' type of yard. Such places have an outward appearance of being an incredible mess of leaky sheds, discarded frames, chocks, old engines and little nests of tools hid in corners. In spite of the outward appearance they can get an amazing amount of work done.

The proprietor of all such yards will have a pair of spectacles which are a little wide on the sideframes and slip down his nose as he leans forward. Thirty minutes in the hour will be spent in adjusting the focal plane of the glasses or looking for a tool when the ensemble is out of focus, the remaining thirty minutes will be incredibly good value.

If the yard is of 'man and a boy' status you should not dream of asking if they will slip the boat, lift the engine and fix a wobbly

engine bearer, and while she is up scrub off and repack the stern gland. Such a request would smack of far too much work in one consecutive run and would be parried with a blank refusal or 'Sorry, couldn't possibly tackle that till October time.'

As he will only have one slipway the first task is to get your boat to the top of it, and he will then be rather stuck until it goes down again. So you might start with 'just slip her to have a look at the stern gland'. Once slipped, ask Mr Bodge for his considered opinion about your engine bearers. Giving opinions is a favourite pastime of small yards, and you will soon be standing around the engine listening to a vitriolic attack on the sanity and skill of the designer and builder (limited to the designer if he or his Dad built her).

The lad will be sent for a couple of spanners and in no time flat your engine will have been demolished and laid in pieces all over the boat (don't try and tidy it up – there may be method in his madness). Two new engine bearers will then be cut out from a huge chunk of timber and the operation will go a bit squiffy when Mr B. leans over the saw bench. You are also a little worried that there is clearly the drawing of someone else's keel on the piece of timber being mutilated.

Amazingly the two new bearers may be rough but fit, and Mr Bodge will then tell you how you should glass these in. Decline any knowledge of fibreglass but compliment him on his amazing catholic knowledge of the boat business. Flattery applied in the right dose will soon have him and the boy mixing up some resin in the ration of about half a potty full (they have some reject children's plastic potties they bought cheap for glass work) to a bit more than a single Scotch of catalyst with a dash more 'cos it's cold today'. The bearers and glass will be sloshed together with a very resin-rich mixture and an untidy stew where they have used several pieces of glass together. As it begins setting you wonder how explosive styrene gas really is as Mr Bodge lights his pipe and surveys the result, which is heavy, untidy but effective.

Whilst you thank him warmly, you both know the job looks a mess, and the sooner it is covered by an engine the better it will look. After a cup of unbelievably strong tea provided by Mrs Bodge you, the lad and Mr Bodge re-assemble the engine in thirty-five minutes. The two washers and three nuts left on the cabin sole defeat you all, but the engine seems to be a runner and fairly well aligned. You retire to a heap of cotton waste and another cuppa. All you have to do is to get her scrubbed and back in the water.

'That's marvellous, Mr Bodge. I don't know what I can say to thank you, etc. etc. Now we have got a minute perhaps you can do an invoice and I will pay up and deal with the VAT and so forth.'

The last remark is the lever. The blood drains from Mr Bodge's face. He has managed to convince the Excise that he is not worthy of club membership, and his office and paperwork are at the end of the bench covered with two clamped-up glueing jobs and at least six months in arrears. The whole concept spoils a day which otherwise had been immensely satisfying for him.

Throw him a lifeline quickly. 'Well don't worry about that. We can tot it up roughly. How much do you charge for a slip these days? Well how about the glass and timber?'

Mr Bodge

A carpenter's pencil is produced to do some sums involving the cubic measure of timber and the unbelievable cost of same and you can see the drift coming to about £120. Before Mr Bodge has caught up with your sums produce some dirty banknotes and start counting and throw in, 'Tell you what, make it £130 and give her a scrub before she goes back.' This will be accepted before anyone works out how much hard work the boy is going to have to do first thing in the morning.

Quite incidentally, the small boatyard technique is the same that you need to get a meal ashore if you have a big crew. Trying to get a table for eleven will only result in your walking round town five times drinking too much on an empty stomach.

You split the crew and go into a restaurant and ask for a table for five. When this is set up seven of you go in to sit down. You pretend to imply that either you or the manager cannot count, but after standing around for a bit you will either be moved to a larger table or two more chairs are produced. You then order wine which seems, and is, excessive for seven. The remaining four then drift in to say 'Hullo, fancy seeing you', 'Have a glass of wine', 'Why not stay and join us for dinner?' The manager or owner is annoyed, flustered, but having been lumbered with you will try to make the best of it by reminding you when he presents the bill how much he has put himself out on your behalf.

Yours, etc.

Dear David,

BUILDING

The notes about boatyards last week refer of course to repair work. If you sell *Lassitude*, building a boat is quite a different project, and you have to steer your way carefully through commercial problems of agreeing to buy a boat at such a low price that the yard go bankrupt in the process, up to an open cheque arrangement whereby all the otherwise unbooked labour in the yard ends up against your new boat.

The concept of a nice boatyard is of a stooped little man with bib and brace overalls wandering around with a beautifully fashioned and seasoned piece of timber wondering where to put it. Sadly, a modern boat cannot be put together with that style, and there is little romance now in rolling on layers of strand mat and resin.

Fortunately there have been more people who have lost money trying to make a living in the marine trade than those who have profited, and it attracts people more for their love of boats than of profit. Such enthusiasm results in more than a fair share of characters who make the game more interesting, such as people who will build you a boat on a fixed price but not send you a bill for several years after you have taken delivery. When you press them hard enough you will get the nicest of all boating letters which goes, 'I think you asked me to build a boat for you a few years ago, and as far as I can remember I said we would do this for about £10,000. In the event Mrs Blodwin who does the books says this comes out at about £18,000 and I cannot understand this, but I know you to be a gentleman, and would be grateful if you will let me have your note sometime.'

Another great character was David Hillyard who built super cruising boats, and found that boatbuilding was a delightful occupation but that owners and potential owners were capable of being rather tiresome. For nearly fifty years he therefore fostered the image that he would only build a boat for you if he liked you (and was capable of deciding he did not like you halfway through and sell it to someone else). This meant that for most of his business life he had prospective customers fawning at him and not daring to lose his favour whilst their boat was a-building. Clever.

The one great problem with all boatbuilders is that none of them will give you any real idea when they will finish the boat. When they want your order they will conveniently forget the work in hand and the other orders they have promised, and once you are committed hope to keep you sweet until they can get round to the job.

As the whole yard knows that they will not get the work when asked in January if they suggest starting in September, it is very hard to get to the truth of the matter. The only hope is to find the lady who cleans the office and buy her a couple of port and brandies. After a third you will find out within a week when your boat is likely to be started and finished.

Major Knowles once had a boat built on the East Coast. He had waited for the start for six months without being notified that much was happening, and thought that he ought to pay a visit to the yard to see how far they had got. Armed with Mrs Knowles and his daughter they drove into the yard, and the manager spotted them and collected up the whole staff to flee through the back gate and have a pint or two of management meeting until they could think of a good explanation as to what was not happening.

After inspecting a deserted office, Sweaty and tribe went for a tour to find their boat. In one of the sheds a lad was swinging an adze more like a croquet mallet and taking chunks out of a plank in the style of an Indian carving a totem pole. He had obtained this job as he was the son of a very important client who had been foisted on the yard manager for his summer holiday. The manager had passed him on to the foreman shipwright who had decided that the razor-sharp adze might cut off a few toes and would be the quickest way to get the lad moved into the design office.

'Is that the keel of our new boat?' enquires Sweaty.

It seemed as likely an explanation as any. 'I think so Sir,' says the youth, who in truth does not know what it is.

'Ah,' says Sweaty to his daughter, 'you need to look carefully at that – it's a skill you won't see in a few years, passed on from father to son. Ah yes. What he's doing is to notch down to the line of the keel and then fair it off to the curved shape.'

Mrs Knowles came up to the group and whispered to Major K, 'There's a boy behind the door rolling around holding his tummy. Do you think we should see if he needs any help?'

Yours, etc.

Dougal McDougal

The yachting letters of Uncle Adrian would be incomplete without some mention of the many missives that were exchanged between us about the 'paid hand' who was meant to look after *Lassitude* – one Dougal McDougal. Paid he was by the Anglo Arabian Oil Company. Hand he tended to be only in helping himself to lift alternate glasses of whisky and beer from the bar counter to the McDougal boiler front.

The truth is that this became the only point of abrasion in the running of *Lassitude*, when in fact Dougal McDougal really was a severe liability. He did nothing whatsoever himself to the boat, could start a strike in any boatyard if *Lassitude* was in for repairs, lose sails that were meant to go to a sailmaker, start a number of fights after a unilateral argument in a bar, and generally walked round with an incredibly dirty old blue jumper which said '*Lass ude*' and doing a public relations exercise akin to promoting B.O.

Dougal had probably come from a Glasgow tenement off the Sauchiehall Street and had that breadth of mind for which that part of the Gorbals is noted. He liked to give the impression of having antecedents from further north and west, and imagined a Highland Chief should indicate his background with rudeness and by ignoring anyone who was not about to offer him a further dram.

Rumours among Adrian's crew, and my family, as to how Uncle had picked up McDougal were varied, interesting and probably untrue. However neither Uncle or McDougal were telling. It must have been a powerful little connection for Adrian to have put up with Dougal from the early days in China for the next thirty years. They had floated to the surface together after they had both assisted in sinking a sloop; Dougal had then followed Adrian east to become the Chief Engineer to the generating station for Lesser Arabia (a grand title for knowing nothing whatsoever about the bank of six G.M. diesels which drove the generator intermittently in that

State). He had also been the chief brewer and distiller of illicit beverages in the same non-alcoholic and thirsty country, the power station being the cover for this large-scale operation, and Gamul Shan Gin and Rasak Tak Scotch were produced more consistently than a stream of nimble amps. In short, part of the deal in getting rid of Adrian had been the Anglo Arabian also having to pension off McDougal as permanent hand to *Lassitude*, presumably before the Ruler of that now important State went under with McDougal cirrhosis.

You can therefore take your pick of the possibilities: Aunt Emily thought that Adrian had uncharitably put McDougal's sister into a parental state – Nigel, that they had restored a flagging economy in China with a little trading in opium – Brig. Erstwhile Paycore that McDougal had gallantly saved Adrian's life (an unlikely supposition if it had involved McD in any physical effort) – and my theory that Adrian had realized the potential in McDougal many years back and had retained him to unleash on anyone he felt was intruding into his sailing life.

Dougal McDougal had a seagoing career from the time he was passed from a corrective training establishment to an ungrateful Navy. The Navy had used him alternately as a stoker and in various Service establishments picking oakum. Dougal had learned how to do almost every criminal activity in an enterprising Service without being caught, had become very sour, and the ultimate Service skate. His whole life being devoted to an avoidance of work, by the time he was inflicted on me he had perfected the art.

While an expert at running a Crown and Anchor board, brewing almost any form of alcohol, and the ability to find a maritime fence and a brothel in any port within thirty-five seconds of arrival, Dougal had not found it essential to know anything at all about ships and the sea. He would tell other people to tie a bowline, but would not be bullied into displaying that he couldn't do one himself, and he had somehow survived in the Navy and as manager of a power station with a very doubtful ability in reading, which incidentally made anything that came with instructions an almost certain disaster.

Erstwhile Paycore explained that in the early days they had tried taking McDougal sailing with them. By mutual consent this was stopped quickly. McDougal found it hard work, cold and wet. He therefore quickly staged a very, very brave coup by deliberately falling overboard, and in the process of being hauled back inboard put up an act of pain and injury which deserved a full season at the Old Vic. 'Me back, Sur, me back,' pain, agony, writhing, 'You've dun me back in Sur,' and so forth for several hours.

For the next fifteen years any hint of physical labour which exceeded lifting a pint tankard to his lips invoked from McDougal an automatic hand on his middle back and a pained expression that the labour would kill him, 'Of course he would gladly do it if Captain Adrian hadn't wrecked his spine when they were sailing all them years ago,' ad nauseum, until he had been purchased a drink or two in sympathy.

McDougal had thereafter been installed as a shore-based boatkeeper with a little cottage up the hill in Cowes. To save any labour in cleaning or cooking he shared this with the barmaid from the Waterman's Arms whenever there was an R in the month and spread his favours more widely out of season. As none of the ladies seemed to complain about his bad back it can safely be assumed that Dougal either recovered after dark or, more likely, laid on it.

The idea of this part of my inheritance was that McDougal would supervise the maintenance of the boat. This involved him sitting watching any yard labour working, and telling them about the times he had known when there were real craftsmen who could do a job like that properly. Light maintenance involved him opening up the boat and if it needed pumping getting someone to do it for him - 'Ach mon, if I were to move that wee pump handle you'd hear my spinal discs grinding across the river' - and then drinking all the booze you may have left aboard. 'I watch her like a eagle, Sur, but them kids still gets in if I slips off for a few hours.' Trying to get Dougal to store up before a weekend produced a very small box of groceries and an unbelievable bill from a grocer in the town who also held an off sales licence.

Dougal would have been tolerable if his usefulness had been kept in the family, so to speak, but as Uncle Adrian's lieutenant I was also expected to become his keeper.

Dear Uncle Adrian,

I am terribly grateful for all the sailing with *Lassitude*, but please please could we move the boat away from Cowes and leave McDougal there. Last week he became so legless after lunch that he went down to sleep it off in the boat, but fell into the wrong one. I have had a furious response from Sir Andrew Hawes who went off in his boat for a run round to Osborne Bay with his secretary to do some dictation. He was nearly taken with a coronary when McDougal staggered out of his forepeak as I guess he was then well into the penultimate paragraph. Not only is he furious with me but is supplying a case of whisky to McDougal every weekend that Lady Hawes comes over to the Island.

I don't need any money to pay McDougal's fine. The Bench fined him £25 and £10 costs: as you know, he wandered into Grummet's furniture store and climbed into a bed in their show window on the High Street to sleep off lunch. Grummet's are so pleased with the front page pictures in the local press of McDougal with his boots stuck out the end of their bed, and all the reports where Dougal told the Magistrate it was the most comfortable bed he had ever tried and done a power good for his old war wound, that they have kept the story going for another week by presenting him with the bloody bed and a cheque for £50.

The *Hampshire Post* printed his story about how he would have retired years ago on account of his disability but for loyalty to you, and how I need help to sail the boat until you are better and how it is only devotion to you that keeps him going in spite of the pain he gets when the damp gets at his spinal injury. I enclose the wretched press cuttings.

Dear Uncle Adrian,

Thanks for your letter about McDougal.

I do have a sense of humour about him. I have asked him if he would like to go out to Malta to look after you. Subject to the terms he would be delighted and you could get a useful rent from his cottage if we turned to and fumigated it and gave it a coat of whitewash before the next Admiral's Cup season. He said the weather would be good for his back. Just telegraph when you wish him to arrive.

Dear Uncle Adrian,

Fifteen all. I have your telegram. It is unusual for the Postal Authorities to transmit such language. I think we have both got the message. McDougal has been put in charge of the boat store and we will stay at arm's length from the daily disasters by keeping the boat on the mainland for the rest of the season.

*   *   *

Dear David,

HEAVY WEATHER SAILING

Until you have done some sailing to windward in really bad weather it is just impossible to imagine what chaos can be created in a boat in rough water, and certainly this can never be imagined in displays of empty boats in their cradles at Earls Court.

Leaping about, with a rhythm which you just get used to until it changes with a violent break, will create strange effects on the people and gear. The people will tend to get sick once they leave the deck, and the process will speed up if they attempt to cook: the best course is to get from the deck into a bunk as quickly as possible. Gear which was carefully stowed away will quickly become free range and the wet clothing, oilskins and towels will become mixed with an egg, the marmalade and the Scrabble. This mêlée will accumulate at the point of lowest gravitational pull, i.e. in the puddle.

A simple operation like getting a handful of biscuits out of the

*'If Skipper says "we haven't got all day" just one more
bloody time . . . '*

cupboard will involve bracing yourself across the galley space, opening the cupboard with one hand and using the other to hold in the rest of the things; an unexpected lurch disengages you from the 'hold' position and you, half the plates, a dozen eggs but NOT the biscuits fall down across the boat to create a very bad-tempered omelette with the navigator and his charts.

Everything however basic takes much much longer to do: bruises and cuts are acquired in the process. You have to go to the loo: your oilskins are wet, both they and your pants are hard to take off, you achieve your pressing need. In replacing the oilskin trousers the braces catch in the door as you move aft, a lurch spins you round the tethered spot, and you crack your head on the bulkhead and break the braces off the top of your pants.

The pain and frustrations in bad weather make you feel that sailing is a mad mad sport. Twenty minutes downwind or in sheltered water will allow the boat to be tidied up and you all to forget how miserable it had been. Rough weather sailing is therefore most comfortable when you have stopped. Whilst you are doing it try to perform as few evolutions other than steering and sleeping as possible.

Yours

Dear David,

Like selling cars, the modern concept of marketing boats has a large dose of sexual suggestion which implies that a power cruiser or thirty foot sloop will greatly improve a man's prowess and the opportunities to display it. In describing the inside of boats this has created the image that the cosy snug is a refuge from the nasty wet outside, and the snuggery becomes the perfect haven for romance.

'Jane, darling – are you below?'

There is no doubt that the male is delighted to encourage this concept, or that a couple of days' sailing and good health raises his libido, but unfortunately you are stuck with the 'two to tango' concept, and on the other side few sensible girls will go sailing and those that do may not react the same way. They do not tend to be aroused by a couple of days without a hairdryer, bath or curtained windows, and are further discouraged by cooking in a general shambles tinted with an aroma of old food, wet socks and diesel oil.

As you have been conditioned by this generation of advertising I do not expect you to believe a word of this, and only hope that you enjoy the anticipation and the journey sufficiently not to be disappointed if the arrival does not turn out as planned.

Having arranged your weekend with a girl who would 'love to come sailing with you' you should only attempt to do so *a deux*. Taking any of the crew would be a disaster as they would consider this a wasted weekend, and do their damnedest to put you off the whole concept for life. The cookie you have elected will be there for her outward appearance and not for any known sailing skill, and this will be proved as you leave the mooring when she will drop the wrong end of the mooring line in the water and lose a couple of fenders. What you say about this could start to make her very un tête à têtable.

Sod's Law of the sea is likely to make this a weekend of a heavy southwesterly gale with a very cold front, and the voyage to the secluded anchorage you had in mind will make her cold, wash off her eyelashes, and induce a growing feeling that she should have gone to Bournemouth that weekend to see Mummy. If you can either reach the mooring or persuade her to stay aboard on the moorings 'until the weather breaks' you are in for a further disappointment when you discover that a fourteen inch quarter berth will not provide a basis for a truthful letter to *Forum*.

If of course you do find a girl who loves you and sailing, will keep out of the way when you are racing, is not reduced to tears by your chauvinist crew, passes up endless bacon sandwiches at sea and does not mind cooking sixteen lamb chops whilst you go off for a few beers when you reach land, you may feel that you have found the ideal lifetime mate. I have to tell you that statistically such ladies are rare, and worse, that the enthusiasm for playing a cross between Fanny Haddock, Raquel Welch and Florence Nightingale can reach a pitch when they are courting, but regrettably decline rapidly when you are caught.

You may have noticed that in masculine society sex is discussed roughly in inverse proportion to the amount they are enjoying at that time, and the discussion and concept will become wilder the

'*Dear* Forum . . . '

further you sail into the Atlantic. On our '64 trip to America I thought it would stimulate some interest, and possibly create a fillip to the flagging Spindrift-Smith fortune, if I channeled this imagination into a practical form by getting the crew to write one of those really horrific pornographic books which clearly make so much money these days. I set them off on the general concept and Brig. Paycore was made editor in chief. I have no doubt that he will recall this as being one of the most enjoyable trips he has ever had, and if you have ever met Mrs E.P. you will wonder at the man's imagination.

I still have the manuscript, and if you meet a publisher who goes in for this sort of thing you can tell him about a really lusty book with a plot which is roughly of a fifty-four foot ketch which sets off from Falmouth to sail to Newport, R.I. Off the Lizard the foredeck hand discovers seven nuns who have stowed away in the sail bin, and everyone is converted by the time they make a landfall on the Venezuelan coast.

Surprisingly the contribution from Nigel, who for his age has used his brown eyes and long eyelashes to obtain a lot of background information on the subject, was pretty tame and could be taken as a chapter from a St John's Ambulance Corps manual on mouth-to-mouth resuscitation. Sweaty Knowles produced some unbelievable concepts that could only be accepted these days on the basis that he suffered a very disciplined upbringing, and Nosey Hawkes is a High Anglican who admires the purity and sanctity of women, and has to live with the problem that so many of his girl friends have tried to disillusion him.

If you have any trouble with the crew, the slightest hint that you have access to the manuscript will regain control.

Yours ever

Dear David,

Cruising

I am delighted to hear that you are off for a couple of weeks' cruising, hopefully in the general direction of Brittany. No doubt you will let me know how you get on, or otherwise.

The Hornblower stories confirm the total and real concern of all those in the era of sail who became absolutely frenetic to use the wind 'whilst it will serve', from the bargee wanting to work his cargo of hay up-river from Wapping Creek to the Board of Admiralty anxiously watching the weather vane over Whitehall to see that they had the right slant to keep Napoleon on his side of the Channel. There was among sailors a passion to move whilst the wind blew fair and the portents were studied with the same concentration as a eunuch trying to anticipate the likely requirements of his tyrant master.

The will to thrash a boat into the wind for thirty hours is a peculiar product of the racing scene, and any enthusiasm to sail in so much discomfort soon fades when there is no glory in finishing a race, or shame in not finishing. All cruising quickly settles down into the directions you can go across or down wind, and therefore produces the same requirements of the old sailing ships which could only sail in those directions.

If the cruising yachtsman wastes a couple of days getting the engine fixed and the wife, kids and stores aboard, by the time they are ready the gentle breeze they have enjoyed while fiddling around will have turned into a thirty-five knot draft coming straight and cold and seasoned with flying scud from where they were planning to sail.

The experienced skipper will therefore be in an absolute twitter to set off as soon as possible when wind and tide blow right. Having got to the first port he will be tempted not to stop there at all if on arrival conditions are set fair for the passage to Port No. 2, and continued fair conditions will induce him to maintain a non-stop Cook's tour until either his weather luck runs out or the crew mutiny. Some such trips will involve so many stops and calls that no one will afterwards be able to work out how you fitted so many events into the week.

If this drive to 'get round the course' is not maintained you will either get stuck near the first port of call or be based on the pub five miles away from your home port. This same feature of cruising leads to the second trait: that the cruising yotti will start fretting about being able to get home again some time before he has arrived at the farthest point from home, and as soon as he has rounded Ushant the debate on how you may get back in time will impose itself on all further cruise planning.

Enjoyable cruising therefore requires some control, which needs the confidence that if pushed you can go in any direction in any weather, leave yourself a day in hand, and then cease worrying about it. Having relaxed, you can start behaving like the Victorian Navy and adjust the cruise each day by getting out the chart, spreading it between the cornflakes and the coffee, and deciding on progress with the crew. Such a semblance of democracy will greatly please your guests and fellow holidaymakers, but don't of course let this run away with you and have them start making suggestions which force you to go somewhere you have no wish to go to or see, or obstruct you from going where you wish. This can be avoided by introducing into the options tides and weather predictions which direct the planning options your way.

If you are cornered, you have started a democratic process and must see it through. Argue your case, then take a ballot with voting slips cast into your yachting hat, and most important, appoint yourself in charge of the ballot. After studying the slips you proclaim a small majority in favour of your plan, and unless you are playing a hand of 8:1 against, it is unlikely that you will be rumbled.

To go cruising each person will need 250 lbs of clutter as opposed to the 25 lbs of stores they survive on while racing. Cruisers are not weightwatchers and gear will continue to be added to the boat 'in case it comes in handy'. It will attract a large toolkit, a vice for the forepeak, Granny's old sewing machine, an electric drill, fan heater, oil heater, Tilley lamp, a couple of planks for fending off, and another couple for a gangway. The lady cruisers will add a pressure cooker, a steel baking box, an iron, hair curlers, a 12 volt hair dryer, and supplies of food which would have caused imprisonment for hoarding in wartime. Clothes will be sealed in plastic bags, with others for spare sheets, tea towels and long dresses in hanging bags. The children will add fishing rods, mackerel lines, beach balls, snorkel, flippers and half the children's section of the local library. In case fuel or water run short spare supplies will be carried in old jerry cans in the stern lockers to

The racing man and the cruising man

create subsequent confusion as to what should go in or out of each.

If ever this load of gear is winkled out of the boat at one time the weight and amount would flabbergast the owner, not to say the helpers who had to hump it. While it makes the cruising yotti secure to feel he is away in a floating fleet depot ship, not much is really necessary and you should take care to get it out of the boat before you try racing again. If you ever need a 20mm drill just look around any port for the deepest laden cruiser and that boat will be absolutely thrilled to rummage the weapon out and even more thrilled when they find that they can offer you a $\frac{3}{4}$ inch one as well 'in case you need a bit of clearance, old man'.

You will find on your cruise that any attempt at doing the traditional tourist sightseeing will fail badly. In a way, folk cruising in a boat are spending a fortune pretending that they are not on a traditional holiday: a trip to see the castle or the early Norman church will somehow remind them that they are doing just that, and the brush with conventional holidaymakers will make them feel uncomfortable. The walk around the town should ostensibly be for either stores or instant food, and the rest of the propaganda of the local tourist board left strictly alone. A 'pardon' in Brittany will only be appreciated by the choir boys' Mums; no traditional folk dancing could ever match up to or be as funny as the Frimley and Camberley Morris Men; and if the area is full of tourist attractions you shouldn't be there.

The purpose of foreign cruising is to have a good reason to sail in nice surroundings and have sufficient exercise to recover from the bouts of very good food and wine taken either ashore or aboard. The very best programme is to lunch off the beach, sleep in the early afternoon, shop in the early evening and in the process mark down the cafe where you think your currency will be best spent. It requires a very early start to get in some sailing before lunch the next day.

Now you may find that a very good dinner followed by a short burst in the casino and then one or six quick nightcaps can mean that your friends do not take kindly to a planned start with the dawn at 0430. Three and a half hours after they staggered out of the Café du Port they will only think of sleeping for another eight hours before staggering back to the same café. This makes for dull cruising. At the back of the galley locker you should find a very large tin of instant lemon tea. This was a marketing disaster, not least because of its name, 'Arise'. If, however, you make nine cups of steaming hot ARISE in the enamel mugs and pass them to sleepy hands that you drag out of sleeping bags you will be able to get the boat going. Having accepted your superheated offering, your friends have a problem. It is too hot to drink. It is too hot to hold. There is nowhere in a bunk you can put it down. If it does cool down after they have got up it is too awful to drink and they will not want to offend you by throwing it away while you are watching. They will therefore sidle up on deck to tip it overboard, and you can then point out what a superb morning it is and how good the tide is if we want to get over to L'Aber-Wrac'h. A cup of coffee and a promise of a sleep off the beach after lunch will slowly sweeten the pill and make them agree with your plan.

132

ARISE!

Once he has crossed the three mile limit the British Yachtsman tends to change character somewhat, and the metamorphosis is best explained by observing that he will now regard himself, his boat and the rest of the crew as a floating Ambassador for the United Kingdom with just a sneaky dash of 'bull' to maintain the tradition of Palmerston and Gunboat Diplomacy. Watch the latter: he would not dream of pinching a sign off the gate of the Cowes Corinthian Sailing Club but when drunk might swipe the board from the Yacht Club Rade du Brest.

Whilst he would never think of wearing other than jeans or a sweater to drink and dine at the Waterman's Arms, seventy miles south he and the rest of the crew will spend a good hour doing what the American Navy call 'liberty guys to glamorize'. There will be shaving and aftershaving, brilliantine and combs, and then a few drinks in the cockpit while the ladies take twice as long to do about the same, and then a few more drinks to allow the ladies to catch up before the whole party in reefers and dresses wander up to Les Arbes des Voileurs for the twenty-five franc menu.

If the lotioning and potioning is done in a fair-sized harbour it will start with a visit to the showers at the yacht club. Although there will be two doors labelled 'his' and 'hers' they will both lead to the same set of showers, and indeed the same old crone will watch the show until her close and active interest is bought off with the accepted *pourbois*. Nothing exemplifies the sad fall of the Pound Sterling more than the fact that if you try and fob her off with 20p instead of local currency she will continue to watch at close quarters.

It may be harder to beat across Lyme Bay to go to the West Country, but the sense of adventure is far greater to do the easier passage to the great 'abroad'. Whilst a trip to Tesco is a chore, a shop around the Belgian, French or Spanish port is not. Most language problems can be solved by pointing to the article required and proffering a handful of the local currency. If you must obtain anything obscure send Nigel who is an able linguist, as trying to buy some sanitary towels for the unfortunate Celia could get you locked up after describing the requirement in mime. Be careful of asking people who know the patois to write down what you want as a short cut to language, and make sure that they do not have an overdeveloped sense of humour before departing with the written instructions.

Be careful of lobsters in France. The French like to hoard gold; if they cannot hold gold they deal in lobsters so be very careful not to upset your economy by meddling in theirs.

Getting in and out of Common Market countries presents none of the problems you might expect from the experiences of dealing with our own Waterguard. Indeed the Customs of the more civilized countries now seem to work a five day week, and in any case regard yachtsmen, quite rightly, as an unnecessary piece of formfilling which, if they ignore for a few days, hopefully and usually will go away. This is not quite the case in Spain where you will be viewed by the Police, the Customs, and the Harbour Authority as an additional member of the British Registered smuggling/Naval/gun running/or subversive community. You should open the ship's bar wide to all visiting officials to avoid being branded as an undesirable or have the Port Medical Officer move you to the Quarantine Berth as a suspect carrier of bubonic plague.

Yours, etc.

The stories of Uncle Adrian's cruises always formed a warm topic of conversation among his old crew. Almost without exception they involved incidents which resulted from anything but the advice in the above letter. The real trouble stemmed from the racing bug Uncle Adrian could not leave ashore when he went cruising, and the quiet little downwind sail he and some friends had planned quickly degenerated into a hairy evolution with a lot of cussing and swearing as they fought to hoist a shy star-cut spinnaker three miles the home side of the Nab Tower.

Not only did Adrian never worry about getting back in time, they always assumed that he deliberately went much farther than the point of no return on the basis that he liked a quiet week in France with his cruising partner while the crew went back to the office for a short week and a double patronage of the Continental rail services.

Though clearly Adrian 'gone sailabout' seldom met with an established level of English Behaviour, he had created a Continental reputation as an English eccentric. Wherever *Lassitude* went we were greeted with variations on a theme of 'Hullo, 'ow ees the Big Idrean?', or 'We has never forgot the night we 'ad with the Adrian for the Bastille, but the new Hotel de Ville is much more, how you say, the fireproof', or 'The man with the circus always ask for your Uncle who come and 'elp put up the cage for the lions and when they finish he and the old General what sail with heem is left on the eenside', or 'Your Uncle is come in with the big gale and is with all the crew up at the Otel with towels on the middle, and that Nigel is given all the wet clothes to take in the taxi to Quimper to, how do you say, the laundrette. He as when waiting too much drinking an fool asleep and then is arrested and the General and Idrean are 'ere for two days in the bathrobe of Madame Sierce at the Café.'

Brig. Erstwhile Paycore summed up all those happy cruises with the notion that 'No doubt, old boy, the French would have given Adrian the Legion d'Honneur but they could never find one of their Generals who was prepared to kiss him.'

Dear David,

English Customs

I quite forgot in telling you what to do in following the *Pilot Book* round the Continent that you also need some skill in returning. This involves firstly stocking up in some foreign port with duty-free stores, and then importing the same into dear old Blighty without upsetting the established conventions formed between the yachtsmen and the Customs service.

It is very hard to justify why we have a Customs service at all: the Americans combine theirs successfully with their Coast Guard; we combine ours with one of raising general revenue from tobacco and brewing industries and collecting VAT. On balance the Americans have the better mixture. If every yachtsman in the country who went abroad came back with a hundredweight of booze and fags the amount of revenue lost to the country would be nothing like the cost of running a Customs service to restrain his imports. Not least because he only drinks the stuff because he could buy it duty free. The Customs of course justify their existence by claiming that this is incidental and that their real function is maintaining the trade blockade on Napoleon, the Kaiser, Hitler, Rhodesia, keeping undesirable drugs out of the country, and now, their latest and greatest justification, to stop yachtsmen importing rabies into a country which does not approve of Hydrophobia.

Even though you may drift in and out of France, Belgium or Holland without let or hindrance, coming into the U.K. means that you are at peril if you do not clear into the first port, and the Customs will come out to you wherever you decide to enter. However, it is quicker and easier to do this as close as possible to one of their little huts, found in every small port. You can do this by lights at night or a yellow flag by day (the latter will mean some sport from the Customs if, after a sail, Celia hangs her yellow bathers up in the rigging to dry).

In a civilized country the officialdom would approach you with considerable apologies for imposing this bureaucratic farce on you. In the U.K. not a bit of it: you are approached aggressively and solemnly to see if this approach makes you crack under the strain, and any proffered refreshment is accepted, but eyed carefully, to establish whether the store from which it was unbottled seemed unjustifiably full.

Having survived the 'third degree' your story about having a bit of this and a bit of that will be accepted, the ship's papers sighted, some forms filled in, and they will part in peace. In all cases, however, they first approach you on the basis that they have the very greatest suspicion that you picked up a full pack of rabid foxhounds at the Outer Spit buoy.

This approach has, of course, nothing to do with catching smugglers, who are all dealt with after tip-offs from the source. The man who sells the half ton of cannabis in Morocco gets a further 25% for passing on details of the consignment and how it is to be landed, the Swiss Bank are on the payroll for an unusual supply of currency, and the jewellery trade feed back details of a large supply of watches as they are unhappy to have their conventional margins eroded. All people who subsidise their sailing by these varied forms of enterprise can expect to be greeted with a team of rummagers on arrival who will systematically take their craft to pieces until they find what they know to be there. As this system works and they seldom demolish a boat without finding what they expect, the rest of the Waterguard exercise with yachtsmen could be questioned, and like village policemen the Customs have to be occasionally moved out of yachting ports back into commercial ones before individuals become converted by the yachtsmen into thinking the same way.

Very keen young Customs who come from commercial ports, the H.Q. of the VAT or from Heathrow Airport can be quite painful to

A pack of rabid foxhounds at the Outer Spit buoy

start with, but are soon tamed into the more civilized habits of yachting by both sides being as difficult as possible until it seems life would be nicer to revert to the normal truce. If they prove untrainable a cassette recording of a pack of foxhounds in full cry played over your deck speaker as you come up any river will get the Customs launch on the water faster than the Lifeboat. After they search your ship for the offending pack several days running you will quickly have the whole town crying 'Woof Woof' when they go into a pub, and they will soon be applying for a transfer back to Kingston-upon-Hull.

Yours etc.

Dear David,

CREWS

The satisfaction of owning a boat is one thing. Ever since man made a dugout canoe it has happened that as soon as he made it big enough for two people he started having crewing problems. The great difficulty of achieving the perfect balance and obtaining, or crewing for, a boat to suit all parties' tastes probably accounts for the great revival in singlehanded sailing in yachts, and solo dinghies.

Like other aspects of life, crews can bring great blessings; they can also be great banes. The crowd you were expecting to sail with you for the Whitsun weekend suddenly remember it's old Bertie's wedding the night before. If you need four or five you will wander between two and ten 'certain if not probables' all next week however carefully you plan it. It is quite difficult enough to organize for red-hot racing boats where there is competition to be in the boat. If you give unlimited hospitality you will attract people, but sometimes not very nice people.

To do the job systematically you need to consider the qualities required in a crew. If you are in a motorboat you need a good engineer – not a mad enthusiast who attempts to rebuild the gearbox off Ushant, but a steady practical type who can fix the electrics by hitting the alternator to make the earth return work, and bleed down a fuel line when the bubbly air somehow gets into the system or the dreaded salt into the filter.

If you want to go sailing you will likewise need a good practical seaman, who is more enthusiastic to go forward and change sails on a wet foredeck on a cold night than you are. For racing you will need a couple of good racing men – not more, as a full boat of experts is a disaster. Build your racing team up round some expertise with keen people who don't know much, but are keen to come out and practice to make that team make that boat go fast.

In all cases you will want to attract a navigator who has had some practical experience and whom you trust, and in all cases you will want a good cook. Not merely a bird who turns out stunning dinner parties off the Brompton Road, but the sort that can do that ashore, and does not need loving care and attention to turn out hot

'What a wonderful day! Why don't you come sailing more often?'

food when the going gets rough offshore. If you find the sort that can do both and also has two sets of everything usual and a nice nature, charm her into the family.

Those are the requirements. Satisfying them is of course impossible. You have to manage with what you can get. They have to manage with you and what you have to sail.

However much you would like a steady group to form a team for most weekends, you will, unless you race hard, find that social pressures make this difficult once your friends get past their early twenties. They will want to sail but have their enthusiasm tempered by family and sweethearts, often leaving one to meet the other over the weekend and using sailing with you as the cover story. Thus about double the number of people to sail the boat is needed so you can rely on about a third to turn up regularly and get the rest with random invitations. Like keeping the boat in good order, this will start taxing your energy as soon as you are back at the office on Monday morning, and you will just get it right by Friday night after a run of alarms during the week.

Yours etc.

Dear David,

Apart from people whom you designate 'crew' who like sailing and like sailing with you, there is another classification of 'duty' guests whom you will feel obliged to ask from time to time.

Such people as business connections, aged parents, your bank manager, or next door neighbour. All will express interest in sailing to please you and confirm that they are not seasick because they made an incredibly rough passage in the *Normandie* once and only they and the Skipper [sic] weren't. Be damned careful not to take them far until you find that you are not risking ruining a business arrangement, cutting off credit, or aggravating a family rift or unspeaking neighbours.

At a party to celebrate the redecoration of the bank (and it needed celebrating) we were making a plucky effort to drink the interest paid on an overdraft for three years in one evening, and the manager, who was trying to be 'with it', was keeping pace. The tide of conversation got round to his maritime experiences as a wartime Mine Watcher. The unexpected bonhomie and hospitality within the normally frightening confines of the bank prompted an invitation to sail to Deauville for the weekend. The crew were contacted and told the unwelcome news that they had to be especially well behaved and nice to Mac the Bank.

We have no doubt that they would have been much nicer to him if he had not been practising what he preached – economy – and had run out of petrol on the A3. This gave the other fifty boats in the race a half hour's start, and the crew's hospitality was noticeably superficial. The golfing jacket, cord trousers and plastic raincoat did not seem at home in the boat, nor did the owner when he was sick for the first time as we got outside. After an exhilarating sail we were subject to that common frustration on the French coast, a foul tide and no wind. Mac the Bank recovered in the hedging and ghosting struggle to get past the French minesweeper and into the lock for tea on Saturday evening.

It did not seem diplomatic to take the custodian of the overdraft

to the Casino – especially in his plastic mac – so we dined modestly. The crew, on finding we had fought our way up to 48th place, went off to get monumentally drunk.

On Sunday morning there was little activity before 10 a.m. and surprisingly no Mac the Bank. A few coffees got most of the crew round a table of toast, boiled eggs and cornflakes when Mac re-appeared looking very pleased with himself.

'Wonderful', says Mac, 'I've found an early Norman church with an apse almost identical to our St Brides' . . . You know I'm treasurer of the St Brides Restoration Appeal.'

A quick attempt to stir the crew into following this theme and developing the conversation on the lines of Church Architecture failed in one. A sullen silence was resumed with occasional crunches of toast and snap and crackles.

'Did you pay for that mirror that got broke in that queers' café?' mumbled a voice still resting its head in a pilot berth.

'I think there's another fine Norman church in Honfleur,' I ventured in desperation.

'Was that before or after the fight?' queried another stretcher case that had not yet made the saloon table.

'We might get a bus this afternoon and look round the church and the castle at Honfleur', I parried as I tried to tot up whether Family Allowance would prevent the pending bankruptcy.

'Who won the toss?' chipped in helpmate No. 2. 'The mother or the daughter?'

'They're just ribbing us.'

'Where did you get to last night, Cecil?'

'The Café Hetrosexique. David thought he was getting off with a real Bridgit Bardot – it turned out to be more he than ha. I did better with his mother.'

Fortunately the wind went south west and light. Mac the Bank and I sailed back drinking a bottle of duty-free; the excesses of the Hetrosexique were slept off.

Sitting in the cockpit with a gentle breeze and a full moon, the two of us decided that Mac had really hated mine-watching – especially when it involved leaving the beach. He wouldn't cruise round the world when he retired after all. He was glad he had found out that he didn't like sailing and would concentrate on getting his golf handicap below 20. I found out that he was a nice chap and didn't really like Norman churches, restoration funds or the bank.

                                                              Yours sincerely

Dear David,

I have your letter about the last two races, but when you are short of crew do not just make up the numbers with a couple of friends who can't sail: all you do is to slow the boat down with a

Leadfoot O'Reilly

142

pair of useless hands and will be distracted while they are being seasick.

You need a couple of heavies who will pull and wind without too much argument, and these can be supplied at short notice by our old Australian foredeck hand Bruce Leadfoot O'Riley. Leadfoot does not sail himself these days, but has settled down in some comfort to live in England just off Eaton Place. He likes to think he is still a dinkum boy by keeping company with the ever-present crowd of Australian Rule rugby players who are over in the old country and also know that Leadfoot may fit them up with either a bird or a bit of sailing for the weekend. Leadfoot's organization is known as 'Rentastrine' and all you have to do is to let him know where, when, and how many. He trips over to the bar where his current supply is waiting; details the two nearest the door who are also sober enough to be playing two-up and can follow his instructions.

Though the Rentastrine process may seem casual, you will invariably get first class hands from him, but the two adopted will keep you guessing by arriving seconds before your departure and have the minutest bag of sailing kit you have ever seen (which they share between them) and a case of Fosters each. If you are lucky one will be able to understand you and vice versa, the other will understand you not and vice versa. Both of them, incidentally, will be called Bruce.

You will have to get Bruce No. 1 to translate to Bruce No. 2. 'Bruce, would you mind asking the other Bruce if he could kindly set up the downhaul on the main boom.'

'EARBRUCESKIPWANSYERTOWACKRUPAKICKER ANDSOCKERDOWNYEBOOMVANGMATE.'

Surprisingly, this will work far more effectively than you could ever get the same chore organized in English.

All Bruces will be strong, so strong in fact that if told to start pulling or winding something they should also be told to stop before the handle bends or they pull the head of the sail through the block or the track out of the deck.

They will prove great fun and you might think that they should be invited to join the crew on a regular basis. They will accept your offer willingly, but the contact number will turn out to be a pay telephone on the landing of a large Edwardian house in Earls Court. The charming New Zealand girl who answers this will tell you she does know several Bruces, but she thinks they were the Bruces who went off last Wednesday in a converted London taxi to the Munich Bierfest.

You replace Bruce and Bruce as required by going back to Leadfoot for another Bruce and Bruce. Your new Bruces will have just come back from a cultural tour of Europe which took in a conducted trip round 119 breweries and the Munich Bierfest. When they go off with a cheerful 'SEEYERALONGNEXTWEEK THENOKCOCKER' you can be sure that a call to their London base will elicit that they have just driven up to Scotland for a visit to a selection of West Coast distilleries.

Dear David,

Some weekends sailing are pleasant, calm and peaceful. You can't really judge the calibre of crew until the stakes get high and things get nasty. We sailed one season with a very nice chap who bounced around with enthusiasm and made everyone cups of coffee, and even if he was not yet a Yotti he was certainly worth having around.

Owing to a miscalculation on the part of the Meteorological Office one race turned into a very aggressive maritime survival course and all sorts of nasties happened. Our coffee maker seemed to be doing well when he suddenly burst into tears followed by very un-Yotti hysterics. A distinctive feature of Adlard Coles' classic *Heavy Weather Sailing* is that it omits to tell you what to do with a hysterical cook – so, for that matter, did our First Aid book. For sure it is an additional problem you don't need with crashing seas and a strong inclination to take up golf all round you.

After a quick conference (aspirin didn't seem to fit the bill) Nigel took the initiative (his great uncle had been a Naval Surgeon and he fancies himself with a mile of bandage and some lint). He approached the patient and whispered into the hysterical ear. It was some months before Nigel would mention what the remedy had been: the hysterics had stopped after the first sentence. He had apparently been told this his ailment was of great concern to the rest of the boat, but after lengthy medical discussion we did not, right there off Ushant, have a remedy handy and that he could either belt up or Nigel and Spud would be forced to use the only anaesthetic aboard – a winch handle.

Yours, etc.

How Nosey Said He Started Racing
There was one well known ocean racing team which had started its career on the East Coast and gravitated, like many others, to the South. Individually the crew might not have been termed charming, but they were Characters. Together they were a very dangerous bunch.

After a week racing round the cans during Cowes Week they came back to Gosport on the Friday evening to fill up with water, booze and food before the start of the Fastnet. They took a very wet dinner in the Gosport

Hilton (the Black Cat Café) and between dinner and the pub closing decided they would need an additional member of the crew for the 625 mile race. Several telephone calls woke various friends and friends of friends, without success.

The race started at 1000 hours: the boat needed to leave Gosport at 0730 hours. At 0725 the nastiest of the crew came out of the toilet and saw a nice young Army officer taking an early morning stroll round the marina with his dog and mother.

'Like a sail, mate? We're one short. Just going off for a jolly.'

'Very kind of you, if Mummy will walk Pekesy, I'd love to. Thanks awfully.' 'Yes, Mummy, I'm sure I'll be home for lunch.'

Complete with umbrella, brown hat and standard Brigade of Guards dog-rubbers, he was hustled aboard and introduced as they cast off. In the mêlée off Cowes before the start he suggested it was great fun, but ought really to be getting back. At the ten minute gun everyone got busy sailing and any further comments were greeted with 'Shut up' or 'Get your foot off the weather sheets'. By the start they had forgotten his name and for consistency dubbed him Orifice. He had another try off the Needles, and another as they took the tide off Portland. The news that he was having a free sail to Eire and back dawned at sunset.

Mummy, his Colonel and Orifice took it very well. He has been ocean racing ever since.

Dear David,

The corollary of Nosey's début is the many stories of people who have started sailing by turning up in a marina at a suitable time before a big race and gone round asking for a berth. This is invariably rejected and the more successful approach has been to observe the boat which is involved in the greatest panic and quietly throw your bag aboard just before they cast off. They will not try to land you and further confuse the start when they are already late, and after a perhaps frosty initial reception your initiative will be treated well and you'll probably be asked again if you make yourself useful.

I am not sure whether the classified advertisement 'Crew wanted, female, young – no experience necessary' actually works for any purpose. Most crews are put together from friends, friends of friends, and friends of friends of friends. Except on the direct connection you will not know if they can actually perform as promised until you have a sail. A lot of potential crew tend to oversell themselves and lead you to expect something akin to the Ancient Mariner – the danger signs show when they turn up and start off acting with incredible enthusiasm, rush round muddling up halyards, restow your tool kit and nearly get all the stern lines wrapped round your propeller. They trot out a series of nearly correct expressions and blunder about the deck 'sorting' everything too quickly into the wrong place. Invariably this burst of energy will be spent quickly and you are left likely to have either a very sleepy or seasick hand on yours by dusk.

The more reliable approach is a rather shy start: 'Where shall I put this, Creeper?' . . . 'Is the blue and white on your main halyard?' . . . 'I'll stay out of the way until you've got her going.'

*　　　*　　　*

Dear David,

Among the many many frustrations of Crews and Crewing problems, there is one great blessing.

It is certainly true of our lives, and probably of most other peoples', that one makes very few lasting friendships after school, university or the Services, and those you make in your early twenties. There is, however, something magical about sailing which allows one to make new lasting friendships throughout life with people with whom you sail. Probably the confines of a small boat tightly restricting the outside pressures, and the sense of having achieved something, or overcome adversity, or sharing a great and exhilarating experience – whatever it is, these bonds can and frequently are made.

Not in the same way that people go on holiday together on an island or cruise ship and for that fortnight become incredibly intimate; the wives swapping details of their sex lives within minutes of meeting, and the husbands at the end of ten days talking about the worries and stresses of their business lives instead of the first nine days of striking an image of how well it is all going. Towards the end of the holiday addresses and telephone numbers are exchanged with solemn promises of visiting each other, and so forth. It never works, even if the assignations are kept: the relative lives afterwards are so different the only thing in common remains the holiday, which by then has palled into a distant memory. You talk about the other people on holiday and that is the end of that.

The friendships made within the confines of a small boat are such that the camaraderie created can continue throughout life. As well as the experience of that wonderful week on the Brittany coast, you will always have a thousand or so words to exchange about the Yot and the Yotti, the Snotti and the non-Snotti.

Some of the most wonderful stories about the sea are written (but not widely known) by Jan de Hartog. In one of his books he tells the story of his ship meeting up with a priest on his way by bike to the Holy Land to try to renew the one moment of total spiritual contact with his God. This had happened when the priest had been an Army Chaplain in the war and was parachuted into the jungle to join some of Wingate's Chindits. He had become entangled in a tree and lost his gear, but had met up with a detachment of his force. In the middle of the night this small group, surrounded by Japanese troops and sick with fear, had gathered round the Chaplain in a cluster, and in a whisper he had given then Communion. A tin mug and water had served as a chalice, a broken up doughnut as the wafer. The effect on the Chaplain had been the most powerful experience of his life: he had felt in total contact with his Maker.

The Chaplain had written to his Bishop to report this spiritual uplift, and in the way of matters temporal within the Church had received a reply which pointed out that Army Chaplains on active service should observe regulation KR21965/32 CofE.Sup. and Communion should only be administered in regulation, and properly consecrated, vessels.

Whatever Yotti churchgoing you aspire to, or otherwise, there will be times when you have had a wondrous day's sailing, or made a splendid passage, and in the words of the Prayer Book have reached 'the haven that you would be.' Your crew tidy up the boat after you have anchored and a very good meal of lamb chops is washed down with many good bottles of Muscadet. You continue with the Muscadet after dinner while you play liar dice, and when you look around the tired but happy faces of the crew you will suddenly know how that Chaplain felt in the jungle.

An unbelievable bill for work on the boat from the boatyard will make you realize how he felt when he got the reply from his Bishop.

Appendix

Self-Examiner in Crewing Technique

by **Major Sweaty Knowles**

As any student of women's journalism will tell you, a quiz is the most useful space-filling device ever invented by an editor (apart, of course, from the full-page colour advertisement). In fact many women's magazines would appear to consist of little else. It must be admitted that *Yachting Monthly* does occasionally carry a quiz, but of a far less frivolous nature than those that appear in sister publications: the average yachting quiz is technically instructive and a positive mine of vital information. E.g. 'You are three cables off the Manacles when hit by a violent line squall. You are immediately dismasted. The propeller is fouled by the anchor warp and your liferaft washed overboard. Wind and tide are carrying you down on the rocks. What would you do?' Answers to be sent in by next week, and not more than ten thousand words. An unbreakable polystyrene limber-hole reamer will be presented to the entrant declared the winner. . . . See what I mean about technically instructive?

YACHTING QUIZ FOR SOCIALLY AMBITIOUS CREW MEMBERS

You have been invited on a weekend cruise to Cherbourg by a wealthy stockbroker, who is just as socially ambitious as yourself. You do not know him well, and the rest of the crew are complete strangers to you. You receive orders to join ship at Lymington.
Question 1 – How do you arrive?
  (a) Late
  (b) Drunk
  (c) In a chauffeur-driven Rolls-Royce with a matching set of pigskin suitcases containing, among other things, a full set of evening clothes. You carry a set of golf clubs and pretend to be under the misapprehension that your host had intended to go to Deauville for the weekend.

Question 2 – While casting off, you inadvertently allow the stern warp to foul the screw. Do you:

149

(a) Apologize

(b) Dive into the cold, muddy waters with a knife between your teeth and hack it free.

(c) Shrug your shoulders and say that you are unused to these menial tasks.

Question 3 – Passing the Needles, you mistakenly refer to the lighthouse as the Eddystone. You are immediately corrected. Do you:

(a) Apologize

(b) Blush and go below

(c) Look affronted and go into some long rambling story about a friend of yours called Edward Stone whose second cousin's next door neighbour knew the man who designed the weather vane on top.

Question 4 – Feeling that you need to make up for your *gaffe* about the lighthouse, you hold forth over supper about your enormous experience in offshore racing. It transpires that the shifty looking little man in the corner is a member of the RORC and sailed in the last Admiral's Cup series. Do you:

(a) Apologize

(b) Blush and go on deck

(c) Hail him as a long-lost brother and begin talking rapidly in a loud voice about your friends, Ted, Max, Arthur, Ron, Owen and Robin and all your contacts in politics, publishing and the building industry.

Question 5 – Nearing the French coast in the early hours of the morning, the navigator succumbs to an attack of hay-fever. The visibility is poor, and the skipper, having heard your yarns of the previous evening and your claims to knowing that section of the French coast like the back of your own hand, offers you the job. Do you:

(a) Apologize

(b) Confess

(c) Sit yourself at the chart table and coolly enquire as to the whereabouts of the radar, the Decca Navigator, the Loran-B, the Omega, the SINS, the satellite fixing system, the . . .

Question 6 – Having tied up alongside the yacht club pontoon in Cherbourg, the heads are discovered to be blocked. Volunteers are called for and you are conspicuous by your absence. Do you:

(a) Apologize

(b) Plead deafness, roll up your shirtsleeves, and reach for the Sanilav.

(c) Disappear, and be found three hours later (after the blockage has been successfully, if messily, dealt with) roaring drunk on board a neighbouring yacht.

Question 7 – Feeling slight guilt about shirking the afternoon's plumbing project, you offer to take the skipper and crew out to a slap-up dinner at the Café de Paris. You order the most expensive dishes, wash them down with gallons of the best wines, behave abominably, insult the waiters, and throw food at the clientele. When presented with the bill, which resembles the National Debt, you realize that you have no money with you at all. Do you:

(a) Apologize

(b) Throw yourself on the mercy of the court

(c) Slip the skipper a treble Calvados with your left hand and remove his wallet with your right.

Question 8 – Feeling something akin to Lazarus the following forenoon, you decline an invitation to accompany the skipper and crew for a morning constitutional before sailing. Unbeknown to you, the skipper's wife, who is some years her husband's junior, has also decided to stay behind with the intention of using the portable shower stowed in the heads compartment. Answering a clarion call of nature, you run full tilt and nearly naked into the heads at the exact moment of the skipper's return. Do you:

(a) Apologize

(b) Faint

(c) Re-adjust your underwear and offer to introduce the skipper to your cousin Erstwhile Paycore's best friend who knows a man whose girl friend's godfather once had tea on the Royal Yacht Squadron lawn.

Question 10 – You set sail for Merrie England. There is a fresh southerly wind and by the time you have passed the breakwater the yacht is bowling along under the influence of main, stays'l, spinnaker, and big boy (the last named sail hoisted at the instigation of the shifty looking little 'rork' man who has been regarding you with utmost suspicion since mid-Channel on Friday night). The skipper is also bowling along under the influence and abruptly goes below, leaving you at the wheel. You immediately gybe all standing – extremely violently. The sails were by Hood. The mast and spars were by Sparlight. The Crockery was by Spode. Do you:

(a) Apologize

(b) Offer to start the engine

(c) Preserve your sang-froid and remark that that was the first williwaw you have encountered since you last rounded the Horn.

Question 11 – The wreckage is tied up in her berth at Lymington. The Customs officer (young, keen, beady-eyed) has just cleared the remains of the yacht and crew, when you accidentally drop the skipper's duffel bag on the deck. There is a smashing sound and the bouquet of fine brandy mingled with the smell of damp French tobacco permeates the air. Do you:

(a) Apologize

(c) Turn Queen's Evidence

(c) Assume a trenchcoat and soft hat, flash a reversed Access card at the Customs officer, and whisper 'Special Branch'.

Question 12 – The constabulary are taking your skipper away. Do you:
  (a) Apologize
  (b) Say, 'See you next weekend.'
  (c) Ask him if you can borrow his Jensen while he's inside.

SCORING: *(a)* counts as –1   *(b)* as 0   *(c)* as 10.

If you can fiddle your score in excess of 100 you are showing a streak of crooked genius and are ready to move on to new sailing grounds – preferably several hundred miles removed from the South Coast. Socially, you are a success, providing you change your friends every few days.

A score of 0 throughout shows consistency and staying power better suited to a more strenuous pastime: we would suggest match standard raffia work.

A score of –12 (i.e. all apologies) shows a definite aptitude for politics: there are plenty of vacancies for yachtsmen at present.

*   *   *